WHAT

Every 4th Grade Teacher Needs to Know

About Setting Up AND Running a Classroom

Mike Anderson

CENTER FOR RESPONSIVE SCHOOLS, INC.

All net proceeds from the sale of this book support the work of Center for Responsive Schools, Inc., a not-for-profit educational organization and the developer of the *Responsive Classroom*® approach to teaching.

The stories in this book are all based on real events. However, to respect students' privacy, names and many identifying characteristics of students and situations have been changed.

ISBN: 978-1-892989-39-0
Library of Congress Control Number: 2010927986

Cover and book design by Helen Merena
Photographs by Jeff Woodward and © Alice Proujansky and Peter Wrenn.

Thanks to the teachers and students of Mary C. Dondero Elementary School, Portsmouth, New Hampshire; Mount Pleasant Elementary School, Nashua, New Hampshire; Kensington Avenue Elementary School, Springfield, Massachusetts; Six to Six Magnet School, Bridgeport, Connecticut; and Wissahickon Charter School, Philadelphia, Pennsylvania, who welcomed Center for Responsive Schools to take photos in their classrooms.

Center for Responsive Schools, Inc.
85 Avenue A, P.O. Box 718
Turners Falls, MA 01376-0718

800-360-6332
www.responsiveclassroom.org

Fourth printing 2017

CONTENTS

Knowing Fourth Graders

Fourth graders are so alive! For good or bad, fourth graders care deeply about almost everything that happens at school, and ambivalence is rare. When I taught this grade, I got used to students rushing down the hallways from the bus in the morning. They would unload their backpacks and coats in a frenzy (often dropping them unintentionally on the floor in their hurry), push through the door, and rush to the schedule posted on the wall. Even well into the year, they'd comment on the day with exclamations of delight and pangs of anguish. "Yes! We have PE today!" one student would exclaim while high-fiving a buddy. "Hey, no fair! You said we were going to get to work on our science projects today!" "We have an assembly later? What's it about? Do we have to go? What if it's boring? I can never see at those things!"

Whether expressed as joy or anxiety, emotional intensity is a hallmark of fourth graders. Exclamation marks seem to pepper their language. School goes best for them when teachers respond to their intensity with a consistent, relaxed, and light-hearted approach. Teaching fourth graders is about creating a safe and comfortable classroom climate so that students feel secure enough to relax and take academic risks.

My goal in writing this book is to provide you with the essentials of setting up and running a fourth grade classroom so that your teaching—and your students' learning—can be joyful and rigorous. You'll find information on everything from arranging classroom furniture to planning and teaching lunch and recess routines, from building community to engaging parents in classroom life. Whether you're new to teaching or an experienced teacher switching to fourth grade, you'll find helpful information and advice about teaching this grade with success.

1

Know Where Students Are Developmentally

As educators know from researchers and their own classroom observations, children's growth and development follow certain patterns. Just as children's height, weight, and physical abilities change, so do things such as their attention span, their sense of humor, their tendency to prefer large or small groups in social settings, and their sensitivities to change, risk taking, and friendship challenges. Knowing our students in these areas that so deeply impact their learning is fundamental to teaching them well. When we design classrooms, lessons, curricular projects, and routines according to our knowledge of students' strengths and needs, we create classrooms that allow students to be more successful, both socially and academically.

I remember my first year teaching fourth grade. I knew that we were supposed to practice multiplication facts as part of our math work, so I set up a system of weekly Friday math quizzes. I started to pressure the students to study math facts as part of their nightly homework so they could do well on Friday. As the year went on, I noticed that some students seemed to be getting more and more anxious. Friday mornings were pure torture for the students who, try as they might, just couldn't memorize the toughest facts. (You know the ones: 7x6, 7x8, 6x8, 4x8, etc.) Not only that, but an alarming number of students started to exclaim, "Oh! I hate math! I'm so stupid!" That ultimately pushed me to drop the weekly quizzes and stop the math fact pressure.

It wasn't until a couple of years later that I learned, from reading, talking to colleagues, and attending teacher workshops, to think about where students are developmentally when trying to understand their classroom behavior. I picked up practical strategies for adjusting my teaching to match their strengths and challenges. I had many "aha" moments as I gained some answers to why my earlier approach to teaching math facts didn't work for many

When we design classrooms, lessons, curricular projects, and routines according to our knowledge of students' strengths and needs, we create classrooms that allow students to be more successful, both socially and academically.

fourth graders. I learned that fourth graders tend to be self-critical and intense. Though they can enjoy competition, the pressure of intense testing and too-high expectations can defeat them. No wonder there were so many tears!

With this realization, I changed my approach. I had the class play games that helped them practice math facts. All students also kept personal multiplication charts in their math books so they could refer to them as they worked on longer multiplication and division problems. I gave an occasional fact quiz to "check and see how we're doing as a class," but the pressure was low. Not surprisingly, some students still mastered their facts easily, while others struggled. However, the stress level in the class was much lower. Best of all, I no longer heard students saying they were no good at math simply because they couldn't remember a few math facts!

Common Characteristics of Fourth Graders

As that last story about math facts illustrates, one of the most commonly recognized characteristics of fourth graders is their intensity and inclination to be self-critical. Fourth graders tend to be sensitive, industrious, curious, and serious about fairness and justice. It's not uncommon to see a group of fourth graders on the playground spending more than half of their recess time arguing about who gets to pitch in kickball or whether someone was fouled in basketball.

The table on pages 5 and 6 details some of the common characteristics of fourth graders. As you use this table, keep these points in mind:

■ **Human development is complex.** Even scientists who study it do not yet fully agree on the means by which humans grow socially, emotionally, linguistically, or cognitively. Most theorists describe the process as involving a dynamic interaction between a person's biological disposition and many other environmental factors—from the historical era in which a person grows up, to the person's culture, family, and the institutions he or she encounters (like schools, places of worship, and the media). The table is not intended to ignore this complexity but instead to offer you a bridge between theory and the reality of classroom teaching.

- **Every child is unique.** As a result of the complex and dynamic process of development, no two children—not even identical twins with the same genetic make-up—will develop in the same way or at the same rate. Also, a given child may develop in one area much faster than in another. For example, a particular fourth grader might display the reading and writing abilities typical of most fourth graders while being relaxed and easygoing when working through conflicts on the playground, a trait more common in fifth graders.

- **The table gives you a practical frame of reference.** It lets you prepare for fourth graders and have a resource if something puzzling comes up. For example, you may notice that many students are melting down during competitive games. This is pretty common in most of the fourth grade year, so you may want to adjust the games to deemphasize competition, knowing that students will probably be better able to handle competition at the end of the year or in fifth grade.

This table is not intended to limit your thinking about students' potential or to lead you to ignore the needs of students who differ from other fourth graders. For example, although many fourth graders can be socially anxious, some thrive on getting up in front of others to perform skits or present research projects. In fact, most fourth graders can be successful with these sorts of tasks if we set them up for success through building a safe classroom community.

To learn more about child development, see the resources in the "About Child Development" section on page 109.

Fourth Graders

Common Characteristics	School Implications
Social-Emotional	
■ Individualistic and competitive.	■ Assign partner work when possible; this minimizes the long debates and arguments that large-group projects may trigger.
■ Often worried or anxious.	
■ Complain about fairness and hurt feelings.	
■ Critical of self and others.	■ Watch carefully for over-competitiveness and criticism of peers.
■ Often prefer same-gender friends.	
■ Need lots of encouragement.	■ Use gentle joking and laughter to help keep things light and playful; avoid sarcasm, which wounds fourth graders deeply.
	■ Lead cooperative and team-building games to build a sense of community and safety.
	■ Keep assessment low-key, concrete, and focused on strengths, not deficits.
Physical	
■ Push themselves to physical limits.	■ Keep students moving to reduce wiggles and help with focus and attention.
■ Complain about aches, pains, and injuries.	
■ May twist hair or bite nails to relieve tension.	■ Allow students to choose their best working position (sitting, standing, etc.) when possible.
■ Better coordinated but still working on physical control.	■ Keep direct-teaching lessons short.
■ Can't sit still for long.	■ If possible, have two shorter recess breaks, rather than one long one.
■ Still need recess and snack.	■ Include snack in the daily schedule.

5

CONTINUED ▶

Common Characteristics	School Implications

Cognitive

Common Characteristics	School Implications
■ Industrious and curious. ■ Beginning to see "bigger world," including social issues. ■ Still very concrete in their thinking. ■ Can draw information from printed material (they've moved from "learning to read" to "reading to learn"). ■ Easily overwhelmed.	■ Elicit passionate engagement by embedding discussion of right and wrong, justice and fairness into science and social studies. ■ Break large projects into bite-sized chunks. ■ Offer hands-on, experiential learning activities.

6

Language

Common Characteristics	School Implications
■ Love word play, new vocabulary, and descriptive language. ■ Sometimes revert to baby talk. ■ Enjoy exaggeration and "dirty" jokes. ■ Very verbal—if they think it, they say it!	■ Use jokes, limericks, silly poetry, and word games for transition activities (standing in line, waiting for assembly, etc.). ■ Tap into students' playfulness and sense of humor throughout the day. ■ Do short skits drawn from their books and stories so they can play with voices. ■ Expect lots of "verbal observations" (*Ew! Cool! I hate that! Awesome!*) during lessons, read-alouds, and projects. ■ Avoid hypothetical questions—fourth graders frequently answer them aloud!

The information in this chart is based on *Yardsticks: Child and Adolescent Development Ages 4–14,* 4th ed., by Chip Wood (Center for Responsive Schools, 2018), and is consistent with the following sources:

Child Development Guide by the Center for Development of Human Services, SUNY, Buffalo State College, 2002. WWW.BSC-CDHS.ORG/FOSTERPARENTTRAINING/PDFS/CHILDDEVELGUIDE.PDF

"The Child in the Elementary School" by Frederick C. Howe in *Child Study Journal,* Vol 23, Issue 4, 1993.

Your Child: Emotional, Behavioral, and Cognitive Development from Birth through Preadolescence by AACAP (American Academy of Child and Adolescent Psychiatry) and David Pruitt, MD, Harper Paperbacks, 2000.

What About Developmentally Younger and Older Fourth Graders?

In any one classroom, you'll find a range of ages. Some years, your class may feel (or actually be) young or old for fourth grade. A group of developmentally or chronologically younger fourth graders are likely to display characteristics common among third graders. Here's just a sampling of those common characteristics, along with suggestions for how you might adjust your teaching accordingly.

Younger fourth graders may:

- **Enjoy socializing and working in groups.** Structure large group projects such as plays or team science projects, and expect that students will socialize as they work.

- **Have still-improving hand-eye coordination.** Allow extra time for practicing handwriting, drawing, and crafts.

- **Have rapidly expanding vocabularies and love to explain their ideas.** Provide lots of opportunities for students to explain their thinking through structures like partner chats and small group discussions.

- **Tend to work/play hard and tire quickly.** Keep periods short. A couple of quick recess breaks are better than one long one. Keep lessons succinct and vary the activity levels of the day. (Follow up a quiet time like writing with a more active one like hands-on science.)

If you have developmentally or chronologically older fourth graders, they're likely to show some common fifth grade characteristics. Following are a few examples and implications for your teaching.

Older fourth graders may:

- **Generally be content, working well in groups and enjoying peers and teacher.** Leverage their social strengths by structuring plenty of group work, book buddies, peer conferences, and whole-class projects.

- **Be experiencing rapid physical growth.** Keep furniture and seating in the classroom spaced apart to help avoid accidental bumps and spills. Offer as much outdoor time and physical challenge as possible, balanced with quiet rest periods.

- **Be good at memorizing facts, classifying, and organizing.** Now you can expect them to master those math facts. Assign more complex science and social studies projects. Incorporate statistics, facts, important dates, and famous people into lessons.

- **Have strong listening and talking skills.** Make use of students' increasing abilities to verbalize their thinking by structuring plenty of class discussions, debates, reading and writing conferences, and math groups.

How to Use This Book

You can use this book in a couple of ways. For example:

- **Read it cover to cover.** If you're reading this book the summer before you teach fourth grade, you may have the time to read it from beginning to end. This will give you the "big picture" of how to set up and run an effective fourth grade classroom. You might take notes as you go, or even use your plan book to make specific notes about how to arrange the classroom or set up the schedule at the beginning of the year.

- **Right now all I need to know is . . .** It may be the day before school starts, and you were just hired or transferred. You don't have much time, and you need to arrange the furniture in your classroom. Or, you may be in the middle of the school year and have a particular challenge (perhaps about communicating with parents about homework or about how to structure a big project effectively). Flip right to the appropriate chapter and skim through until you find what you need. You can always go back and surf around a little more when you have the luxury of more time!

Regardless of how you use this book, consider implementing new ideas slowly. Just as we shouldn't overwhelm a student with several big changes to make all at once in one writing conference, we need to be gentle on ourselves. Try one or two new things at a time and get comfortable with them before moving on to new changes. Don't worry about making mistakes. The best teachers are also the best learners—ones who try new ideas, make some mistakes, learn from them, and try new ideas again.

Ready? Get Set …

Fourth grade is fantastic. I truly love the spirit and energy of fourth graders. They're in this magical time when they aren't really "little kids" anymore, but they haven't hit adolescence either. Primed for learning and craving positive adult attention, fourth graders will quickly become immersed in their learning and passionate about their work when given a safe and comfortable classroom atmosphere.

I'll never forget Shawn, a student of mine who illustrates fourth graders' potential to connect with school. Shawn was an athletic and active boy who had never really loved school before fourth grade. At one parent conference, his mother, a strong and forceful woman, sat down with me and immediately demanded, "What's happened to Shawn?" Taken aback, I asked what she meant. Her tone softened as she gave me a wink. "We were at his brother's baseball game last night, and he asked to stay in the car because he wanted to write some more poetry. I've never seen anything like that!"

How could you *not* love teaching fourth grade?

Go!

> *Don't worry about making mistakes. The best teachers are also the best learners—ones who try new ideas, make some mistakes, learn from them, and try new ideas again.*

CHAPTER 1

Classroom Setup

Setting up the physical classroom with the typical characteristics of fourth graders in mind can profoundly impact your students' ability to learn. Often anxious, these children need a good measure of security in their classroom starting from the first day of school. Knowing where to sit, park homework, and get supplies reduces worry and lets fourth graders concentrate on their learning.

In my fifteen years of teaching, I've tried many classroom designs and observed many colleagues' classrooms, learning essentials about setting up a classroom for fourth graders. In this chapter, you'll find guidelines on choosing and arranging furniture, gathering and storing materials, and creating classroom displays. You'll also find tips on using technology with fourth graders. Besides allowing you to set up a classroom that gives fourth graders the support and security they need to do their best work, these guidelines will also help ensure that the learning in your classroom is active, interactive, and child-centered—important in any grade.

Arranging the Furniture

Early in my teaching career, I'd spend hours and hours every August arranging and rearranging the classroom furniture. Should I put desks in clusters? Where should the meeting area go? Should the bookshelves line the walls or come out from them? I lost count of the number of hours I spent tweaking the classroom layout. Gradually, through experimentation and seeing what worked in other teachers' rooms, I settled on the following methods of furniture setup that have served fourth graders' learning needs well year after year.

11

Whole-Group Circle

A whole-group circle is the most important area in any elementary class-room, and fourth grade is no different. This is the first area I set up every year. The circle is perfect for the three-part lesson structure that works so well for fourth graders: brief whole-group instruction in one or two specific skills (done in the circle); a longer stretch of active and interactive learning (done at students' desks or tables); and finally a whole-group closing in which children share reflections on their work as a class or with partners (done in the circle).

The circle is also a great place for the class to meet briefly each morning to greet one another and warm up for the day ahead. Gathering in a circle, where everyone can see and be seen by everyone else, sets the tone for a friendly and focused day of learning. I find that starting every day with a *Responsive Classroom*® Morning Meeting is a great way to fulfill this purpose. Whether or not you hold a formal morning meeting, having a circle area allows you to gather the children for similar activities to build community and launch the day.

Learn More About Morning Meeting

The Morning Meeting Book, 3rd ed., by Roxann Kriete and Carol Davis (Center for Responsive Schools, 2014).

If your classroom is short on space, try to get a little extra room for a circle by trying new arrangements for the students' desks or tables. (See "I Don't Have Room for a Circle!" on page 14 for more ideas.)

Points to keep in mind:

- **Allow enough space.** You need an area big enough for a circle that lets a whole class of fourth graders see everyone else. Remember that fourth grade bodies can be big, and they're growing rapidly. Your circle (even with younger children) will often become more like an oval or rectangle, so keep an eye out and adjust the space as needed.

- **Use chairs if possible.** Chairs give each student a defined space, which helps with self-control. Chairs are also more comfortable for many students this age, and that comfort helps them focus. If your classroom is small, have children sit on the floor to save space.

- **Assign seats in the circle at the beginning of the year.** You could write students' names on a piece of masking tape attached to each chair or post a seating chart showing students' spots in the circle. Knowing where they should be will help students feel a bit safer. As the year progresses, you can work with students to develop a list of fair and inclusive strategies for choosing a place in the circle.

13

"I Don't Have Room for a Circle!"

Unfortunately, this is not an unusual dilemma for teachers. Here are some possible solutions:

1 Create a temporary meeting area.

At meeting time, the children move desks and other furniture to open up a large space for a circle. After the meeting, the students return the furniture to its original place. With adequate teaching and practice, children will be able to do this setup and takedown in just a few minutes.

Three keys to making a temporary meeting area work:

- ■ **Choose carefully.** Choose a spot with as little furniture as possible. Any furniture should be easy for students to move.

- ■ **Use props to define the area.** An easel pad typically works well. Ideally, the easel pad would stay put and serve as the point from which the meeting circle grows.

- ■ **Teach furniture moving.** Use Interactive Modeling to teach and practice how to move the furniture carefully, cooperatively, and quickly. Try turning the practice into a game, such as beating the clock.

> **Interactive Modeling**
>
> See Chapter 2, "Schedules and Routines," for a full explanation of Interactive Modeling.

2 Create it once, use it twice.

Have children move furniture to make room for a circle at the end of the day and gather the class for a "closing circle," in which the children reflect on their day, share about their work, or plan together for the following day. After the meeting, leave the space open—don't move any furniture back. The next morning, the space will be ready for a meeting that welcomes the children, affirms the strength of the community, and warms them up for the day ahead. Once the morning meeting is completed, the children move the furniture back. At the end of the day, they repeat the process.

3 Use a space outside the classroom.

Go to the cafeteria, library, gym, or other space in the school that's large enough to accommodate a circle. This solution, admittedly the most challenging, works best when you:

- **Use the same space every day.** The familiarity will help children succeed.

- **Limit distractions.** For example, if you use the cafeteria, meet when no other class is there.

- **Meet at the same time every day.** Even if it's not the most ideal time, the predictability will help students focus and feel secure.

- **Teach the expected behaviors.** Be sure to teach transition routines and behavioral expectations outside the classroom.

The whole-group meeting circle is the heart of classroom life. Sitting in a circle, everyone can see and be seen by everyone else. And because the circle has no beginning and no end, it allows everyone an equal place in the group. By the very nature of its design, the meeting circle invites group participation and fosters inclusion. Its presence and prominence in the classroom or in the school day, even if only temporary, say "In this classroom, we value working together, and we value each individual's contributions to the group."

Desk and Table Seating

When you use the circle area as your main space for direct teaching, students can use their desks or tables primarily as work spaces. Arrange the desks or tables and seat students in ways that enable fourth graders to work most productively:

■ **Spread out.** Spread tables out around the room. If you use desks, cluster them in twos and threes. Having space around them and proximity to just a few classmates helps fourth graders relax and concentrate. You can put clusters against the walls (try attaching desktops to the walls on hinges if you're pressed for space; fold the desktops flat against the wall when they're not in use). You can even work a cluster into the classroom library area.

■ **Assign seats.** Use assigned seats to give anxious fourth graders a place to call their own starting from the first day of school. Mix genders to let students know you expect boys and girls to work together, and periodically change seat assignments to give students practice working well with all of their classmates.

■ **Consider student needs.** When assigning seats, consider whether certain students need to be near certain others (for example, a particularly anxious child might need to be near a friend; a child struggling with self-control may need to be with others who are not easily distracted).

Fun Ways to Assign Seats

■ **Card sort.** Write students' names on cards. Every other week, place the cards randomly into groups and have students move to their spots for the following two weeks.

■ **By interest or hobby.** Collect information about students' interests at the beginning of the year. Create interest-based groups.

■ **By commonality.** Place students with others who have the same number of siblings, who were born in similar places or in the same season, or any other commonality that you glean from a "get to know each other" survey. Once they're grouped, invite students to try to figure out the category!

■ **Be proactive.** Head off seating-group problems before they start. When creating groups, ask students, "When you move to your new groups, what can you do to be friendly to your new groupmates?" Keep an eye out for cliques or quiet negative-talk about others. Move students when necessary.

■ **Consider free seating later in the year.** As the year unfolds, you may decide your students are ready to choose their own seats. This can be incredibly empowering for fourth graders and can provide valuable lessons in sharing space. But before setting them off to choose, carefully discuss how to make good choices (being fair and inclusive, thinking about where you need to sit if you're easily distracted by the science supplies, etc.). Then be ready to monitor choices and redirect when necessary.

When Spreading Out Doesn't Work

If you're not able to create even a temporary circle area, put desks and tables in small clusters in the middle of the room so students will be able to comfortably see you and any visuals you're using. Be sure to give students lots of movement breaks. For an occasional change of scenery, once you've finished your direct teaching,  let students spread out to work on the floor or in any workable space they feel comfortable using.

Work Standing Up? Give It a Try.

Gregory, a fourth grader I taught, was always moving. His legs bounced when he sat. He twirled in circles while standing in line. He ran for twenty minutes nonstop at recess and came inside dirty, sweaty, and still bouncy. To ask Greg to work sitting down would've been torture (for him and for me). He needed to stand. I have vivid memories of Greg working on math, standing at a table shifting from foot to foot, kicking himself in the behind as he worked. Since Greg worked productively that way, and it didn't bother anyone else, I let him continue.

Different children will find different work positions comfortable. Some, like Greg, may want to work standing. Others may prefer to grab a clipboard and sprawl on the floor or sit leaning against the wall or a floor cushion. If you can let students work in their preferred positions, the whole tone of the room may become more mellow.

Other Areas of the Classroom

Besides the circle area and desks or tables, you'll need a classroom library, areas for writing, science, and computers, and storage space. To fit all these in, think about designing multipurpose spaces. The following chart shows a few spaces that can be easily used for more than one purpose.

Area	Tips	Multiple Uses
Circle area	■ Make the area large enough for the whole class to gather comfortably, sitting in chairs or on the floor ■ Include an easel for teaching and for recording children's ideas	■ Morning and other meetings ■ Whole-class lessons ■ Space for reading, writing, and other work on the floor ■ Small-group instruction while others are working ■ Whole-group activities and energizers
Classroom library	■ Arrange bookshelves with enough space around them so that many students can browse at once ■ Try a horseshoe shape so the bookshelves create a cozy space big enough for a table or cluster of desks	■ Book display and storage ■ Guided reading, if you include a table ■ Conference area ■ Regular work space ■ Team project area
Writing supply area	■ Stock with pens, pencils, markers, paper, sticky notes, dictionaries, and thesauri ■ Post graphic organizers and writing tips from focus lessons here	■ Writing supply storage ■ Writing display area ■ Writing conferences or general work space, if you include a table

Area	Tips	Multiple Uses
Science supply area	■ Set up a tank of murky pond water or a terrarium with bugs caught at recess; add some note sheets, magnifying glasses, and field guides, and you've got a science center! ■ Spur other science investigations by supplying batteries and bulbs, a big box of building set pieces, or kits of rocks and minerals	■ Ongoing tinkering, observation, and exploration area, regardless of what science unit you're studying ■ Indoor recess; students will gravitate to this spot on rainy days ■ General work space, if you include a table
General storage areas	■ Periodically clear out worn or damaged supplies or things you don't use often	■ If you have freestanding bookshelves or storage cubbies, put hooks on their backs for hanging coats and backpacks
Computer area	■ Arrange computers so that the children can easily move keyboards and mouse pads	■ When the computers aren't in use, students can use the computer tables as work space for reading, writing, math, or other table work

Classroom Supplies

Fourth graders can do incredible work when given appropriate resources. Here's a typical day in my class. We're studying different states in social studies. Andre is busy near the sink making a clay replica of Mount Rushmore. Nearby, Melissa, Mark, and Anthony are using watercolors to create portraits of famous people from the states they're studying. Elsewhere in the room, Demetri is using craft sticks to recreate his state's statehouse, while Anna is graphing the population changes in her state using a meterstick, large oak tag, pencils, and colored pencils. The learning throughout the room is focused, varied, and rich.

Having a variety of quality tools and materials is crucial to achieving this kind of engaged learning. That's why it's so important to invest some thought into choosing and managing classroom supplies.

Three Keys to Keeping Your Classroom Well Supplied

No Budget for Supplies?

If your school does not give you a supply budget but instead relies on parents to provide supplies, you could replace the traditional shopping list with assignments so that each parent donates one category to the class. For example, one parent supplies the pencils, another some markers, and so forth.

Also, you could explore using a website set up to link interested donors with classrooms:

- WWW.DONORSCHOOSE.ORG
- WWW.ADOPTACLASSROOM.ORG

- **Variety.** Having a wide choice of supplies encourages fourth graders to do creative and thoughtful work. Children of this age are gaining fine motor dexterity and are eager to learn new craft and project skills. Supplies like calligraphy pens, wax pencils, and modeling clay can challenge and delight fourth graders, adding vigor and engagement to their work.

- **Quality.** Fourth graders can be very self-critical, so they need quality supplies that enable them to do good work. Scissors need to be big enough for their hands and sharp enough to cut. Staplers need to staple easily and properly. Markers need to be fresh and moist, with caps to keep them that way.

■ **Quantity.** Having quality materials won't do much good if you don't have enough for the children to share easily. For competitive fourth graders, three pairs of nice scissors mixed in with twelve junky pairs will become the source of arguments. If only one black marker works well,

Making Supplies Last the Year

Having enough supplies reduces arguing and hoarding. But having too much can lead to wastefulness. Consider rationing things like construction paper, drawing paper, and erasers. Leave enough out so there's plenty for all, but tuck some away for later in the year. Otherwise, you'll run out by mid-winter!

students will sneak it into their cubby so they alone can use it later. Having a sufficient amount minimizes these predictable flashpoints.

Great Fourth Grade Supplies

The following chart shows examples of supplies to have in a fourth grade classroom, along with quantities for selected supplies. This is not meant to be an exhaustive list, but rather a starting point. Although the supplies are grouped by category, clearly many materials could fit in multiple categories.

Good Supplies for a Fourth Grade Classroom

Category	Early in the Year	Later in the Year	Sample Quantities
Art, social studies, projects	■ Crayons ■ Colored pencils ■ Markers (thin and thick) ■ Drawing paper ■ Construction paper ■ Magazines (for cutting from) ■ Yarn ■ Craft sticks ■ Glitter ■ Toothpicks ■ Glue ■ Felt ■ Tape	■ Calligraphy pens ■ Wax pencils ■ Oil pastels ■ Paints ■ Stencils ■ Modeling clay ■ Hot glue gun ■ Papier-mâché supplies ■ Colored tissue paper ■ Wire ■ Pipe cleaners	■ Scissors—one pair for every two students ■ Glue—one bottle for every two students ■ Markers, crayons, colored pencils—an ample supply for each table or desk cluster ■ Papier-mâché supplies, tissue paper—bring out less often, and rarely for the whole class; quantity depends on how many students will use these, and how often
Literacy	■ Books, both fiction and nonfiction, multiple genres ■ Sticky notes ■ Paper for rough and final drafts ■ Pens, pencils ■ Staplers ■ Writing notebooks/ journals ■ Clipboards	■ Books (new genres; keep cycling in new books throughout the year) ■ Highlighters ■ Note cards ■ Binders ■ Clear plastic portfolio sleeves	■ Books—a wide assortment, many in multiple copies ■ Pens, pencils—several dozen of each ■ Staplers—two good ones for the class to share

Good Supplies for a Fourth Grade Classroom

Category	Early in the Year	Later in the Year	Sample Quantities
Math	■ Rulers ■ Calculators ■ Base ten blocks ■ Pattern blocks ■ Graph paper ■ Variety of math games ■ Dice	■ Protractors ■ Compasses ■ Cuisenaire rods ■ New math games ■ Fraction puzzles	■ Rulers, protractors, calculators—one for every child ■ Pattern blocks, base ten blocks, Cuisenaire rods—large containers for small groups
Science	■ Science notebooks ■ Building sets ■ Magnifying glasses ■ Bug jars ■ Field guides	■ Microscopes ■ Batteries, bulbs, etc. ■ Other hands-on materials that match your curricula	■ Enough for partners or small groups
Recess (indoor and outdoor)	■ Math/logic games ■ Literacy games ■ Trivia books (also good for those few minutes when the class is lined up waiting to go to lunch or an assembly) ■ Jump ropes ■ Playground ball, football, basketball ■ Jigsaw puzzles	■ Mad Libs ■ Board games (quick ones like Boggle, Yahtzee, etc.) ■ Computer games ■ Fun websites ■ Snow brick makers ■ Sidewalk chalk	■ When supplies are limited, such as with playground balls and computers, consider a rotating sign-out system so all students have a chance to use them

See appendix for favorite books, board games, and websites for fourth graders.

Community Supplies Only

In my first couple of years teaching fourth grade, I was surprised by how much students argued about who owned which supplies. "Nicole, can I borrow your black marker?" Carradine would ask. "No. My mom bought these for me." Carradine would push, "But you're letting Rachel use your markers." Nicole would shrug and Rachel would reach over and take the black marker.

Of course, we had an ample supply of markers (and other materials) in the room, but the ones from home often seemed especially desirable. And the "private" materials presented other challenges: Some students would have better supplies than others; some would loan materials to their best friends only. Someone would accidentally break a friend's ruler, and an argument would ensue about who should replace it.

Finally, a colleague suggested having community supplies only. Students would bring in supplies from home only if they were willing to donate them to the class for everyone to share. Instead of getting a list of required supplies to purchase for their child, families would receive a list of supplies they could purchase for the class if they wanted to. All supplies would be kept in community bins for everyone to use, and everyone would have access to the same supplies for their work. If students had special supplies they didn't want everyone to use, those would stay at home for project work done there.

What a transformation this made in our classroom community! A more peaceful atmosphere prevailed as the children bickered less and worked more.

If you're going to try having community supplies, make sure to communicate with parents so they know why you're using this system. Some parents might be confused and even upset if there isn't a list of supplies to get for their child. I found that parents were very understanding if I explained my goals for having community supplies: building a strong community, making sure all students would have access to high-quality supplies, and helping children learn how to share and cooperate.

Location of Supplies

Letting students keep large quantities of supplies in their desks is a recipe for lost and broken supplies. It can also tempt students to use the supplies at inappropriate times.

Effective ways to house supplies in a fourth grade classroom:

- **On tables.** If students generally sit in desk clusters or at tables, place often-used supplies in the middle so everyone can reach them. Coloring supplies, pens, pencils, paper clips, sticky notes, and rulers can all fit easily in supply caddies or large cans.

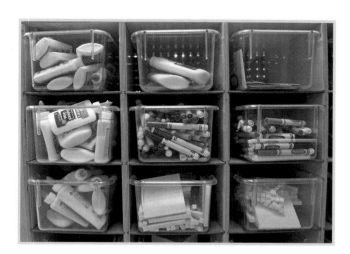

- **On shelves.** Keep materials like glue, staplers, and scissors in larger bins in a designated supply area. When students need something, they go to the supply area, choose what they need, and bring it back to their work area.

Classroom Displays

Displays of Student Work

In a fourth grade classroom—as in any classroom—displays should consist primarily of work the children themselves have done. Displaying student work

sends several important messages: *As teachers, we value what students do. This is their classroom as much as ours. And in this classroom, students share their work, learning from each other.* Furthermore, students will look at their own work more frequently than at commercial posters.

Some things to remember about displaying student work:

- **Display in-process and polished pieces.** Displaying unfinished work sends the message that we value the process of learning, not just the products. Encourage students, for example, to proudly put up writing pieces with cross-outs and highlighter marks. This helps anxious fourth graders see that it's okay for learning to be messy and that mistakes are part of learning, not things to hide or avoid.

- **Use wall spaces for two-dimensional work.** Display paintings, writing samples, book reviews, and other two-dimensional work on bulletin boards and other wall spaces.

- **Reserve bookshelf tops for three-dimensional work.** Keep the tops of bookshelves clear for dioramas, models, and other three-dimensional pieces.

- **Consider adding simple shelving.** Use simple wire shelving from a hardware store along portions of walls to create more display space.

- **Keep displays current.** Take down old work and reference charts from units that are finished.

Informational Displays

In addition to display spaces for student work, you'll want to create some space for important reference charts and information. Bulletin boards should change continually, right along with the content you're teaching and the time of the school year. Some anchor charts (posters reminding students of lessons or key ideas and facts they should remember) may change often to reflect current learning. Other anchor charts will stay up all year as reminders. Ideally, the boards and charts will be centrally located for easy student reference.

Some good fourth grade informational displays:

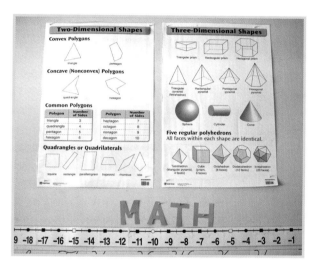

■ **Get-to-know-each-other board.** At the beginning of the year, post everyone's name (and picture, if you can) on a board with lots of space between the names. As you learn about students (Jeremy has a dog, Margaret likes to swim, Rico was born in the Dominican Republic), post information bubbles next to the names.

■ **Birthday chart.** Posting everyone's birthdays for easy reference boosts students' sense of belonging in the classroom.

Control Clutter!

■ Take down displays that are no longer relevant. Walls cluttered with charts and papers can appear messy and add to the stress levels in the room.

■ Leave ample blank wall space around bulletin boards, anchor charts, and student display spaces.

■ **Word walls.** Post current and relevant content-specific vocabulary and commonly misspelled words. Reduce anxiety by including words fourth graders generally find tricky (such as *people, girl, because*).

■ **Content boards.** Include interesting facts, maps, and pictures for each content area. Add new items to the board slowly (one

or two per day) and make a big deal about each new item by sharing it with the class in a dramatic way (saving a special few minutes of the day for a "grand opening," for example). Remove older items to avoid overwhelming your fourth graders. To make content boards interactive, invite students to add their own pictures that fit the theme, answer questions, or solve riddles. For example, if you're studying state geography, you could invite students to find pictures of each state's landscape in newspapers and magazines or on the Internet to post on the bulletin board.

■ **Process or format reminders.** Is there a certain way students should sign and date their work? Is there a process they should use for turning in homework? Do you have criteria for good work that you expect all students to meet? If so, create some simple charts and hang them where needed.

■ **Routines charts.** Have charts to help students know how to sign up for lunch and how to sign out to use the bathroom. Have an attendance chart that students fill out posted by the door. Finding ways for children to be independent with these little routines can make for a much smoother day.

■ **Anchor charts from lessons.** After teaching a lesson, post a chart of a few of the key ideas that students need to remember. You might post an example of how to solve a long division problem, or a few key ideas about building a riveting opening to a piece of fiction. As students work, they can refer to these anchor charts to help them as they practice new skills.

Technology

Used well, technology can bring richness, depth, and energy to fourth graders' learning. Fourth graders will enjoy having ample opportunity to try using various technologies as part of their work. They can use them to design quizzes for the class and presentations for science research projects. They can take photos on a social studies field trip and email them to parents. They can search safe websites for information about a topic they're studying. The possibilities are endless—and sure to increase as time goes on and technology changes even more.

But teachers need to make sure students are using technology appropriately. Here are some basic guidelines:

■ **Decide which tools students can use on their own.** Make sure any tools that students shouldn't handle on their own are safely tucked away. Fourth graders are often just capable enough to get themselves into real trouble. ("Mr. Anderson! I *know* I did everything right, but now this thing won't turn on!")

■ **Monitor technology use.** Properly supervise students' use of technology, including their use of the Internet. Know your school's policy on what is considered appropriate use, teach it to your students, and stay vigilant.

■ **Ask for help.** If you're uncomfortable using technological resources, ask for help from a colleague or parent. Work with the experts in your school to ensure that every child can access the technology resources you plan to use.

■ **Use technology purposefully.** Just because a technology is available or in vogue doesn't mean you have to use it. As with any resource, make sure the technology you use will enhance your efforts to strengthen the classroom community and make learning active, interactive, and child-centered.

Closing Thoughts

Designing a classroom around the needs of fourth graders can hugely impact your students' learning and make school life more productive and enjoyable for everyone. You'll have many issues to consider, though, so don't worry if you can't address them all. None of us can. Instead, choose a couple of ideas from this chapter to try. Once you're comfortable with those, pick a couple more. Each year, setting up a classroom will feel a bit more comfortable as you build on your previous successes and keep tinkering and trying new ideas.

CHAPTER 2

Schedules and Routines

I remember the week before my first year of teaching. I was working furiously to get ready for the start of school. I made sure to plan out how I would introduce writing workshop and had the first math unit planned out. I had a big bulletin board ready, welcoming students to the school year. Materials were organized, tables were washed, lessons were prepared. And then the students entered the room.

"When is lunch? How do we fill out lunch tickets?"

"When can we use the bathroom?"

"What bus am I supposed to take home?"

I was bombarded with an endless stream of questions about procedures and routines, and quite frankly, I wasn't sure how to answer half of them. How *did* those lunch tickets get filled out? Could students just use the bathroom whenever they needed to, or should they sign out first? Did we have to go as a whole class? Weren't the kids supposed to know what bus to take home? Fortunately, the students and I muddled through those first few days and got things sorted out, but we didn't get to half of the academics I had planned.

I learned a valuable lesson: No matter how well lessons are planned and the room is organized, without structures and routines in place to help students take care of the "little" things like using the bathroom, eating snacks, lining up in the hall, and transitioning within the classroom, effective teaching and learning will take a back seat. Teachers need to teach (and reteach) basic classroom routines so students will feel safe and secure. And as I learned in that first year and the years to follow, giving fourth graders a schedule that's as consistent and reliable as possible is also important. Since fourth graders often struggle with change and tend to be anxious, this consistency is a great gift to them.

In the following pages, we'll discuss how to construct a schedule that will work well for fourth graders. We'll also look at a good method for teaching key classroom routines. Throughout this chapter, we'll revisit one theme over and over: Consistency and predictability are key!

Scheduling

The first step in constructing a supportive daily schedule for fourth graders is to think about their needs. The next is to list the components of an average day and then order those components by time slots.

Think About Fourth Graders' Needs

Industrious and intellectually curious, fourth graders are ready to work hard, giving their attention to both the process and the product of their schoolwork. They tire easily, though, and do best when their lessons are not too long, with movement breaks in between to refresh their bodies and refocus their minds for more learning.

Some specifics to keep in mind while thinking about your schedule:

Fourth Graders Need to Move!

■ **Give breaks between work periods.** A ten-minute snack break or a group game outside will help fourth graders transition from one academic period to the next, boost their ability to fully engage in academic tasks, and reduce misbehaviors.

■ **Build movement into the day.** For example, try to put work areas on one side of the room and supplies on the other. Even a quick walk to get a ruler provides a nice movement break that will help fourth graders sit still and focus on lessons or quiet independent work.

■ **Structure movement into work periods.** For example, students could start a math session by working alone, then join partners in another part of the room to play a game, and finally move to a new part of the room to share their learning in teams.

■ **Do fun, two-minute games to boost or calm children's energy levels.** For ideas, see Chapter 4, "Classroom Games, Special Projects, and Field Trips," and also see *Energizers! 88 Quick Movement Activities That Refresh and Refocus, K–6* by Susan Lattanzi Roser (Center for Responsive Schools, 2009).

■ **Stamina.** At the beginning of the year, most fourth graders can handle work periods of about thirty minutes. As their stamina grows, you can try periods of about forty-five minutes, and by the end of the year, depending on the class, you can stretch some periods to around sixty minutes. If you must schedule two such work periods in a row, be sure to put an energizer break in between. (See the box "Fourth Graders Need to Move!")

■ **Pacing.** Fourth graders generally do well with a three-part lesson structure:

1. Several minutes of direct teaching

2. A longer period of working, either independently or in groups (at the beginning of the year, most fourth graders can handle fifteen to twenty minutes of working; by the end of the year, they can often work for thirty to forty-five minutes with great energy)

3. A very brief wrap-up giving students the opportunity to share thoughts on their work

33

■ **Energy cycles.** Fourth graders are primed and ready for challenges early in the day, so consider scheduling their toughest learning then, when their self-control and positive energy are at their highest. By the end of the school day, fourth graders are often exhausted, so saving tough work for the last forty-five minutes may bring on tears and temper tantrums from these self-critical children. Students often love independent reading, so putting reading workshop last can help end the day on a calm and productive note.

■ **Need for varied activity levels.** A day in which they're either too active or not active at all will exhaust most fourth graders. Vary the children's activity levels by trying,

for example, a quiet writing workshop, with students working independently or in pairs, followed by a science or social studies lesson, with students moving around and working in more active groups. This undulating activity level will help students find a comforting rhythm in their work.

List the Day's Components

Include both the academic and social components of an average day. For example:

Arrival routine	Lunch
Reading	Two short recesses
Writing	Snack
Word study/spelling	Read-aloud
Math	Special (art, music, etc.)
Science/social studies	End-of-the-day routine

Order the Day

Although some components may fall into fixed slots beyond your control (specials and lunch, for example), it's still helpful to start with an ideal schedule based on fourth graders' developmental needs and then tweak it as necessary. Approaching scheduling in this way will help keep your scheduling decisions child-focused.

Page 35 shows a couple of ideal schedules for you to adapt as needed.

Easing the Recess-to-Classroom Transition

- **Recess first.** Exercising and then eating fits how children's (and adults') bodies naturally work. When physical needs are met, behavior generally improves. If your school schedules lunch first, you may want to suggest trying it the other way around.

- **Quiet time.** Consider having ten to fifteen minutes of silent independent work time when students enter the room after recess/lunch. They can read, draw, catch up on homework, or work on a math or word puzzle. This quiet time helps children shift gears.

- **Read-aloud.** Reading a good book right after recess/lunch can ease any ruffled feelings and help the group settle into the afternoon. See the appendix for some favorite fourth grade read-alouds.

Two Ideal Schedules

8:30–8:45	Arrival routine
8:45–9:15	Morning meeting
9:15–10:00	Math
10:00–10:10	Outside whole-class game
10:10–10:25	Snack, quiet math puzzles/games
10:25–11:05	Writing workshop
11:05–11:15	Word study
11:15–12:00	Special
12:00–12:20	Recess
12:20–12:40	Lunch
12:40–1:00	Quiet time
1:00–1:20	Read-aloud
1:20–2:10	Science/social studies
2:10–3:00	Reading workshop
3:00–3:10	Clean up and pack up
3:10–3:15	Closing circle (See "Ending the Day with a Closing Circle" on page 44)
3:15	Dismissal

8:30–8:40	Arrival routine
8:40–9:00	Morning meeting
9:00–9:50	Writing workshop
9:50–10:20	Word study
10:20–10:30	Outside whole-class game
10:30–10:45	Snack
10:45–11:30	Math
11:30–12:15	Recess and lunch
12:15–12:40	Read-aloud
12:40–1:30	Science/social studies
1:30–2:15	Reading workshop
2:15–3:00	Special
3:00–3:10	Clean up and pack up
3:10–3:15	Closing circle (See "Ending the Day with a Closing Circle" on page 44)
3:15	Dismissal

Teaching Classroom Routines

Having set procedures for doing everyday classroom business reassures fourth graders and helps each school day unfold smoothly. Because students don't enter school in August or September with all the skills they need to function in the classroom, it's important to intentionally teach routines—even simple ones. Something that seems as basic as carrying a chair may need clarification. Is it okay to grab the chair by its back and drag? Is that loud scraping sound okay? Carrying the chair overhead gets it out of the way, but is it safe?

The more we break down classroom routines and teach each piece carefully, the more orderly and calm the classroom environment. At the beginning of my career, I was so eager to get to "the good stuff" of writing workshop, hands-on science, and math that I often skipped the explicit teaching of routines. As you might guess, I spent huge amounts of time dealing with a multitude of disruptions and misbehaviors. I learned that teaching routines is well worth the time it takes.

Use Interactive Modeling to Teach Routines

Before we get into which skills and classroom routines are most important to teach, let's first look at how to teach these to set students up for success.

Interactive Modeling is a teaching strategy that gives students the opportunity to think about, observe, discuss, and practice the skills needed to perform classroom routines independently. The next page shows what the steps of Interactive Modeling might sound and look like if you were teaching children how to carry a chair safely.

Interactive Modeling: Carrying a Chair Safely

Steps to Follow	Might Sound/Look Like
1 Say what you will model and why.	"When we carry our chairs in the classroom, we need to be safe. Watch while I carry this chair."
2 Model the behavior.	Carry the chair safely. You do not need to narrate as you model.
3 Ask students what they noticed.	"What were some ways I was carrying the chair safely?" (If necessary, follow up with questions such as "What were my hands doing?" and "What were my eyes doing?" to prompt children to list the important elements: used both hands, looked at the chair legs so they don't poke somebody, etc.)
4 Invite one or more students to model.	"Who else would like to show us how to carry a chair safely?"
5 Again, ask students what they noticed.	"What were some ways that Tom carried the chair safely?" The children name specific safe behaviors that Tom demonstrated.
6 Have all students practice.	"Now we're going to practice carrying our chairs safely from the circle to our seats. I'll be watching and seeing you do all the things we just practiced."
7 Provide feedback.	"We were carrying chairs safely! I saw chair legs pointing down, and all of you were using two hands and looking around you as you walked!"

Keys to Successful Interactive Modeling

CLEARLY ARTICULATE ROUTINES FOR YOURSELF

Determine what the skill or routine is and exactly how it should look and sound. "Walk quietly to the door to line up" is not specific enough. What does "walk quietly" mean? Is whispering okay or is silence expected? Should students line up single file, or can they stand in pairs? (I've found that fourth graders appreciate and can handle walking in pairs and whispering while they walk.) Think of possible challenges when children try to follow the routine. For example, where should the line go when it meets tables, desks, or other obstacles?

> **Interactive Modeling and Academics**
>
> Academic skills and routines (lattice multiplication, using proper punctuation, listening attentively) can also be taught and practiced through Interactive Modeling. To learn more, see *The Joyful Classroom: Practical Ways to Engage and Challenge Students K–6* (Center for Responsive Schools, 2016).

KEEP EXPECTATIONS HIGH

Once you've modeled and practiced routines, holding fourth graders to the expectations you've established will help them feel secure while keeping the classroom orderly. If you tell students chairs must be carried a certain way and then allow them to do it differently, you're sending the message that you don't mean what you say. So when you see the class hurriedly carrying chairs over their heads, be firm: "Stop! Everyone put your chair down." Once the class is ready, review: "We weren't carrying chairs safely. Who can remind us what safe carrying of chairs looks like?" Then release: "Okay. It sounds like we're back on track. Try again."

MAKE SURE EXPECTATIONS ARE REALISTIC

Sometimes, in our efforts to create an ideal learning environment, we set such high standards that they become unrealistic. Unrealistic expectations lead to student failure and teacher frustration. Here's a common example: Well-intentioned teachers set a policy of "no talking" in hallways so that learners in classrooms aren't distracted as children pass by. But for many fouth graders, walking and talking go together. Expecting children to be silent, therefore, is unrealistic, and modeling it would only establish a pretty much unreachable standard. Expecting children to walk and talk quietly is realistic, so that's the behavior we should model and practice. Be sure to model exactly what volume of speaking is okay. You might say

"Speak in a voice that's just loud enough for the people near you to hear," and then move into your modeling session.

PROVIDE ONGOING REINFORCEMENT, REMINDING, AND PRACTICE

Interactive Modeling is the critical first step in teaching routines, but it is just the first step. Students will need support as they continue to practice. When the class does well, reinforce their behavior: "Congratulations! You all kept your hands to yourselves when we walked down the hall, and almost everyone remembered to use quiet voices." If a routine has been especially tough for a particular student, you might pull that child aside for a private reinforcement when she or he does well: "Lisa, that was the best you've done at walking down the hall safely and considerately." Keep watching how students are doing and offer quick refreshers when needed: "Who can remind us how to walk safely and considerately in the hall?" Model the routine again if necessary.

Key Routines to Teach

It's important to begin teaching routines at the very start of school—on the first day, if possible. Here are the most important routines to focus on. Remember, it's critically important to interactively model and guide students in practicing each of these routines before expecting students to be successful with them.

SIGNALS FOR QUIET AND ATTENTION

During my first year of teaching, I tried several ways to get the group's attention: shouting above the noise (thereby modeling exactly what I didn't want students to do), flicking the lights on and off (which made the room look like a disco hall), and talking over the class to give directions before they were ready (which caused me to repeat myself regularly because many missed what I'd said).

Finally, I learned the magic of using simple visual and auditory signals to get students' attention. Using these signals helped transform the tone of the class as much as anything else I did. When they hear or see the

signal, students finish their conversations or their work within fifteen seconds, put down any work materials, turn their bodies toward the person who gave the signal, and look at that person.

■ **Visual signal.** Simply raising your hand is a good, simple visual signal. Once some students see your raised hand, they then raise their hands, in turn alerting classmates to finish up quickly and come to attention.

When modeled and practiced well, the raised-hand signal works wonders to get the attention of a group during circle time, when students are lined up waiting to go out the door, or any other time when students can see you easily.

■ **Auditory signal.** The visual hand signal won't always be appropriate, though. Picture a class of engaged fourth graders playing math games. Their heads are close together as they roll dice, record scores, cheer, and groan. They're so wrapped up in what they're doing that you could stand with your hand up for five minutes before anyone happened to look up and see you.

A hand chime or a pleasant-sounding bell can be a good signal for these times, as can a wind chime hanging from the ceiling, a wooden train whistle, a rain stick, or any other nice-sounding musical instrument. The signal should be loud and clear enough to cut through the chatter of busy students, but soothing and pleasant enough to relax nerves.

■ **Student signals for teacher's attention.** Children also need to know how to get your attention. Should they raise their hand, or is it okay to call out? How should they address you (Mrs. Jones, Ms. Jones, Mrs. J.)? What signal should they use if you're talking with someone else and they have a question? Whatever systems you use, make sure to model and practice them a lot!

BATHROOM, SNACK, AND RECESS ROUTINES

Before I even arrived at a recent professional development conference, I found myself searching through the program schedule looking for lunch and snack breaks. As soon as I got to the conference, I scouted out the breakfast buffet and made sure I knew where the bathrooms were. Our students start the first day of school thinking about the same things!

Bathroom, snack, and recess routines, then, are ones to teach and practice early in the school year. It's best to adjust these routines to fit the time of year. By midyear, students may be able to handle a simple sign-out sheet for the bathroom and a "grazing" snack style—eating when they're hungry while they work. But they probably won't be ready for these structures on the first day of school. Beginning the year with whole-group structures for bathroom, recess, and snack routines will be easier for you to manage and more comforting for fourth graders.

The following chart shows how these routines may change throughout a fourth grade year.

How Routines Might Change During the Year

	Bathroom	Snack	Recess
Sept.– Oct.	For the first few days, have students take regular bathroom breaks throughout the day as a class. If students need to go at other times, they may ask. After the first few days, shift to a bathroom sign-out chart hung by the classroom door. Students write their name and what time they left and returned to the room so you can make sure they're not going too often or staying too long.	Plan whole-class snacks with assigned snack tables. Give clear warnings for finish and clean-up times.	The first six or so weeks of school is a great time to play together as a class on the playground. Teach tag and other running games and join in or actively supervise. This lets you build community, model and practice appropriate recess behavior, and make sure everyone's included in recess. See Chapter 3, "Building Community," for some favorite fourth grade tag games.
Nov.– April	Once students show they can use the bathroom responsibly, let them simply use a hand signal or head nod to let you know they're going. If you have an older class, the signal may work earlier in the year. A young or challenging class may never be ready for this much independence.	Consider shifting to a "grazing" snack in which students can eat as they work throughout the day. Most fourth graders can handle this approach, though it must be well taught and closely monitored.	Your class may be ready to take over the responsibility of organizing group games themselves each day. Or they may only be able to handle it a couple of days a week. It often depends on the personalities and social dynamics of the class. Fourth graders' competitiveness often erupts on the playground, so continue to join or directly supervise their play whenever possible.
May– June	Some classes may need to revert back to a more structured system such as a sign-out chart as they struggle with the impending transition into summer. The structure will soothe those worrying about next year or already missing the sense of safety that school offers.	As with the bathroom routine, independence with snacks may be harder as the end of the year rolls around. You may find it better to reinsert a regular snack time into your schedule to help students cope with year-end stress.	Just as group games build class cohesion at the beginning of the year, they also help at the end, when children may begin to feel sad about leaving their classmates and teacher for the summer.

READ-ALOUD ROUTINES

I'll never forget running in after recess when I was in fourth grade and sliding to a stop at Mrs. Mottram's feet, ready for the afternoon read-aloud. There's just something about listening to a great book after lunch! Some of the many fantastic books out there tie directly into the content we need to teach (*Sign of the Beaver, The Witch of Blackbird Pond,* and *Sarah, Plain and Tall* are just a few examples). Others are just fun. The following suggestions will help you choose books and make sure that read-alouds work well. (See the appendix for other possible read-aloud books.)

- **Alternate books with male and female protagonists.** If you've just read *Because of Winn-Dixie,* whose main character is a girl, try *Maniac Magee* next. Also consider the gender stereotypes that may be embedded in books. Although I love *The Chronicles of Narnia,* it does have some gender stereotyping. Be ready to talk with your class about this as you read.

- **Consider books about fairness.** Books like *Frindle* and *Matilda* appeal to fourth graders' sense that sometimes grown-ups are unfair. Great class discussions can emerge as you discuss what's right and what's fair in such books.

Ending the Day With a Closing Circle

A "closing circle" can be a calming and focused way to finish a school day. Instead of students standing in line (or worse, wrestling on the floor!) as they wait for buses to be called, consider having the class gather for quiet reflection or a relaxed game in the day's last minutes. Here are a few ideas for closing circles:

■ **Partner share.** Students chat with a partner for a minute or two about something they enjoyed from the school day.

■ **Around-the-circle share.** Each student gets to say one thing he or she learned or practiced during the day.

■ **Favorite game/song.** Is there a favorite math or spelling game the class enjoys? How about a relaxed and enjoyable song they love? These can be fun and relaxing ways to finish a day.

■ **Look for books with challenging and playful language.** I usually read books that many of my students struggle to read on their own. This gives me a chance to push their vocabulary development while letting all readers experience a rich story with complex characters and content. I also choose books that have playful language, such as those by Roald Dahl.

■ **Set clear expectations.** Fourth graders have a hard time doing two things at once, so be careful before you allow students to snack, doodle, or braid each other's hair during read-aloud.

■ **Think about posture.** I'm okay with students lying down, as long as their heads are up and they look at me so I can better gauge how they're enjoying and understanding the book. I know some teachers let students lie with their eyes closed, and others require students to sit upright. Whatever you decide will work for you, make sure you model and practice it well with your class.

BEGINNING- AND END-OF-DAY ROUTINES

The start and finish of the day are important to any grade, but especially fourth grade, when students can have quick swings of energy and emotion. These are also the times when things can be most chaotic: Students bump and push at the coat racks, homework is turned in or shoved into backpacks, notes from or to parents change hands, etc. There's a lot to do and remember, and fourth graders can be overwhelmed by the many tasks and noisy confusion.

To help students stay calm and organized, ask them to help generate a list of the tasks to be accomplished at the beginning and end of the day. They'll feel more involved in the process of learning the necessary routines if you invite their ideas, and it will also help you better understand how this time of day feels to them. Here's the list of end-of-day tasks that students in one of my fourth grade classes generated:

- Find homework.

- Put homework in the folder.

- Unzip backpack in the hallway.

- Pack lunchbox and homework.

- Check with a friend about Little League practice.

- Find my gloves.

- Check to make sure I know which house I'm going to and that I have a key.

- Remember the bus I'm on.

- Put on my coat.

- Come back to the circle area for a closing circle.

Once your class has generated their list, work with them to generate a general list that will apply to all students. A sample:

45

- Put homework into folder, then into backpack.

- Pack lunchbox.

- Gather coat, gloves, hat, umbrella, etc.

- Which bus do you ride? Listen for that number.

- Think about your afterschool activity. What do you need for it?

- Come to closing circle.

Then model and guide students in practicing any activities on the general list that might need clarification. Copy and post the list in critical areas: over the coat racks, near cubbies or storage areas, etc.

Keeping Things Fair

You can avoid some upsets and resentful feelings by using simple structures to decide whose turn it is to do or lead a routine. A few ideas:

- **Move down the list.** Make a poster of all your students' names. When it's time for the next "fair" decision, simply move down the list: "Mary's next on the list. She'll lead the line today."

- **Choose names randomly.** Make a name card for each student and draw cards randomly as needed: "Let's see, who's going to help pass out paper? Laticia and Jarrod, your cards came up!" Their cards then go into the "Had a turn" can.

- **"Person of the day."** Tell students you'll designate a "person of the day" by rotating through the class roster. Each day, a different student gets to be first to line up, pick recess equipment, etc.

As the year progresses, the class's arrival and dismissal routines will likely shift, just as their bathroom, snack, and recess routines do. Homework routines will change, snow pants may enter the scene, and the bus dismissal time may fluctuate. You can always update the poster as the year goes on.

TRANSITIONS

Ever count how many times the whole class transitions in and out of the room or from one activity or subject to another? Just moving in and out of the room to specials, lunch, and recess requires a total of six transitions. Throw in a special assembly and a trip to visit book buddies and the class could be leaving or entering the room ten times a day, to say nothing of the number of times they'll be transitioning between subjects or activities inside the classroom.

Modeled and practiced so that students are efficient, sociable, and task-oriented, these transitions can actually be positive influences on the day: a chance to stretch legs, a change of scenery that can reinvigorate learning periods. But if not modeled and practiced, transitions can destroy the sense of community, with children shoving and complaining and the teacher chiding everyone.

Issues to keep in mind as you plan modeling sessions:

■ **Racing the clock.** Since fourth graders can be overly competitive, racing the clock can be either highly motivating or distressing. Observe and get to know your students to see if this is a good strategy.

■ **Music.** Soothing music can help children transition smoothly.

■ **Noise.** Teach children to use quiet voices during transitions. Model and practice what a "quiet" voice will be. (I often explain it as loud enough so people nearby can hear, but people across the room cannot.)

46

When teaching transitions into and out of the classroom, think about:

■ **Cleaning up.** Students need some clear guidelines for where to put "in process" work, finished work, and materials and supplies. They also need to know how tables and chairs should look. Posting pictures of cleaned tables or desks and neat supplies around the room can serve as good visual reminders for fourth graders.

■ **Order.** An order that works well with fourth graders is to put away materials, get drinks, use the bathroom, line up.

■ **Lines.** If you lack space for a straight line, decide where the line will turn. Make sure to model the lining-up procedure so students know just what to do. It's sometimes helpful to have a line-order so students aren't spending lots of energy jockeying for position as they line up.

Learn More About Schedules and Routines

The First Six Weeks of School, 2nd ed., from *Responsive Classroom* (Center for Responsive Schools, 2015).

When teaching transitions within the classroom, think about:

- **Space.** If you lack space at cubbies, the sink, and between desks for all children to move at once, divide the group into two. One group starts at the cubbies and the other starts at the sink; then they switch.

- **Chairs.** To make room for traffic during transitions, establish a "push chairs in" rule.

WHAT TO DO IN AN EMERGENCY

Your school probably has fire drill and lockdown routines, but there may be times when you have a classroom emergency. You may need to rush out of the room with a student who is vomiting or has a bloody nose, or you yourself might feel sick and need to leave the room quickly. Have class expectations in place for these moments and practice them ahead of time.

Some ideas to adapt to your situation:

- **Students keep working.** If students are working independently, they just keep working.

- **Students read at their seats.** If students are together in the circle or you are in the middle of a lesson, they get out a book and read at their seats.

- **Someone alerts the next-door teacher.** Designate a student to alert the next-door teacher that you've stepped out or need the teacher to come help you in your classroom.

- **Someone alerts the office.** Designate one or two students to alert the office that you have an emergency.

OTHER ROUTINES

Which routines or social skills you need to teach each year will depend on your classroom setup and your students' needs. Some possibilities:

- Indoor recess

- Taking care of class supplies

- Settling in for read-aloud time

- Greeting classmates or visitors in a friendly way

- Feeding class pets

- Winning and losing a game graciously

- Signing up to use a computer

- Filling out the lunch ticket

- Walking in the hallways

- Asking someone to lend a book

- Turning in homework in the morning

Remember to Teach Recess and Lunch Routines!

See Chapter 3, "Building Community," to learn about these middle-of-the-day routines.

Closing Thoughts

All children, particularly often-anxious fourth graders, are better able to settle down and concentrate on learning when they know what to expect during the school day. Setting up a schedule that acknowledges fourth graders' need for security, variety, rest, and movement will do much to help these children, as will carefully teaching and modeling routines for the daily activities of classroom life. These steps are well worth the time they take. The more you invest in creating a safe, comfortable, and predictable environment, the more productive and pleasurable your classroom will be for the children—and for you!

CHAPTER 3

Building Community

I'll never forget the end of one particularly successful year of teaching fourth grade. Our class was reflecting on our year together, and suddenly Anna piped up, "Mr. Anderson! I don't want our class to split up! We all get along so well in here." "I know!" chimed in Steven. "How come we have to go to different fifth grade classes anyway? It's not fair."

A chorus of agreements followed as the students gushed about how much they enjoyed each other and how they didn't want to leave. I remember smiling (and aching a little bit, too) because I felt the same way. I also remembered that it hadn't always been like that. October had been a mess. Boys and girls had teased each other. A clique of three friends had excluded others both in the classroom and on the playground. There had been endless (at least it felt endless at the time) minor squabbles and arguments about who was supposed to sit where and who had to work with whom. ("Mr. A., Josephine just got up for one second to get a tissue and Mark stole her beanbag chair!" Mark: "No way! She wasn't using it . . . her stuff wasn't on it!")

But at the end of the year, my students were right. They had gelled into a cohesive and tight-knit community. It hadn't been easy, but it was absolutely intentional on my part. Fourth graders, like all children, learn and behave at their best when they feel known and supported by those around them. Building a sense of community in the classroom is therefore a top responsibility for teachers.

In fourth grade, building community is a joy and a challenge. On the one hand, fourth graders can be testy and cranky, hypercritical and overly competitive—hardly characteristics that help them come together as a class. On the other hand, fourth graders can be sweet, loving, playful, thoughtful, and

joyful. Efforts to nurture fourth graders' positive characteristics while moderating their more challenging ones must infuse just about every aspect of the school day.

This chapter suggests ways to craft a tight-knit, friendly classroom atmosphere that will enable fourth graders to learn together as they take the emotional risks necessary for academic engagement.

Teacher Tone and Demeanor

Classroom community begins with the teacher. Our tone and demeanor deeply influence students' mood and tone, which deeply influence their ability to form meaningful bonds with each other. Highly sensitive fourth graders need teachers who are emotionally steady, firm, kind, and upbeat.

Suggestions for setting a positive tone:

■ **Show easygoing acceptance.** Model how to shrug off disappointment and lose games with grace and aplomb: For example, when allowing the class to vote on a recess game to play, you could also vote. If the vote doesn't go your way, you could respond "Oh, well! That wasn't my first choice, but this one will be fun, too!"

■ **Be matter-of-fact about work.** When tests, quizzes, and other pressure-packed learning assignments loom, set a tone of relaxed, purposeful work: "Okay, everyone, remember that we think best when we're relaxed, so take some deep breaths. This test will give us a good chance to see how we're doing as a class on our math work so we can figure out what we know and what we need to practice a little more."

■ **Laugh!** Our lively sense of humor can help ease the souls of tense fourth graders and tap into their love of laughing and playing. Model appropriate jokes and relaxed humor. For example, when lining up for recess, try invitations like this: "Anyone who ate bugs for breakfast may line up."

Greetings

Beginning each day with a greeting is a great community-building strategy. There's something affirming about hearing someone speak your name first thing in the morning. Although greetings typically last only a couple of minutes, they pay dividends all day by expanding the children's capacity to work together respectfully.

The *Responsive Classroom®* Morning Meetings I use with my students begin with every student greeting another until everyone in the meeting circle has heard her or his name spoken in a friendly, respectful way. Early in the year, students may simply turn to the person next to them, look at that person, and say "Hello" along with the person's name. Later in the year, they may add a gentle handshake or high five to their hello. Still later, they may get up and move around to greet several classmates, or add a complex element such as sharing a piece of personal news as part of their greeting.

If you don't have morning meetings with your students, you can still have them greet each other in a sincere and pleasant way that helps everyone feel included.

Tips that will help greetings go well:

- **Set the tone.** Set a respectful and sincere tone for greetings at the beginning of the year. Stress that greetings are an important part of the day—something everyone will take seriously.

- **Start simple.** Begin the year with a simple, low-risk greeting in which each child turns to the next child in the circle and says "Good morning, _____." Gradually introduce more complex greetings.

- **Always model.** Interactively model all new greetings so that students know how each greeting should look and sound (see Chapter 2, "Schedules and Routines," for more on Interactive Modeling).

- **Emphasize inclusiveness.** Ensure that over time, everyone greets everyone else, not just special friends or same-gender classmates. Try building inclusivity into greetings: "Today your challenge is to greet three people you didn't greet yesterday."

- **Guide when necessary.** If students continue struggling with inclusivity, be more directive. Assign seats and do an around-the-circle greeting. Or you might have students pick names out of a hat. You could even go back to a more basic greeting, where students simply greet the classmate next to them.

Good Fourth Grade Greetings

Early in the Year

- Turn and say "Good morning, _____."

- Pass a handshake and "Good morning, _____" around the circle.

- Greet and shake hands with the person on your right and the person on your left.

- Add a quick question to the greeting: "Good morning, Billy. What are you looking forward to doing in school today?" Pass this around the circle.

Later in the Year

- Greet using each other's last name: "Good morning, Ms. _____."

- Try a category greeting: "Greet someone who likes math" or "Greet someone who has a sister."

- Skip count around the circle: "Greet every fifth person."

- Greet someone in a different language: "Buenos días, Charlie!" "Bonjour, Jill!"

- Greet someone different: "Greet someone you don't normally sit with at lunch."

Learn More About Greetings and Morning Meetings

The Morning Meeting Book, 3rd ed., by Roxann Kriete and Carol Davis (Center for Responsive Schools, 2014).

99 Activities and Greetings: Great for Morning Meeting . . . and other meetings, too! by Melissa Correa-Connolly (Center for Responsive Schools, 2004).

Interactive Modeling of Greetings

Steps to Follow	Might Sound/Look Like
1 Say what you will model and why.	"One of our rules is 'Be friendly to everyone.' Today, each person will greet someone else in a friendly way. I'm going to greet Emma. Watch me carefully and listen to what I say."
2 Model the behavior.	"Good morning, Emma." Use a friendly tone, show a friendly face, and turn your body so you're facing Emma.
3 Ask students what they noticed.	"What did you notice about how I greeted Emma?" (If necessary, follow up with questions such as "What kind of voice did I use?" or "What did you notice about my body?" to prompt children to list the important elements: friendly voice, friendly face, body turned to the person, used her name, etc.)
4 Invite one or more students to model.	"Let's have two people volunteer to greet each other in those ways."
5 Again, ask students what they noticed.	"What did Linnea and Ricky do as they greeted each other?"
6 Have all students practice.	"Now we're all going to practice. I'm going to partner you up, and you're going to try greeting your partner. I'll be watching and seeing you do all the things we just practiced."
7 Provide feedback.	"I saw lots of people using friendly faces and voices. It sounded like many people remembered to greet their partner by name. We'll try it again tomorrow to see if we can do it even better!"

Getting to Know Each Other

Helping students know something about all classmates' interests, strengths, and personal lives is crucial to the whole class becoming a strong community. When children know and are known by each other as people, they become connected in deep and important ways. Supporting this kind of connection

among all classmates is critical at every grade but perhaps particularly in fourth grade, when children have a tendency to form exclusive cliques if left on their own.

It's also important that we teachers know our students well. Only then can we form the strong teacher–student relationships that enhance our ability to teach.

Getting-to-Know-Each-Other Activities

At the start of the year, have the class do some activities designed to help them get to know each other. As you devise get-to-know-you activities for your class, keep in mind that good choices are ones that:

■ Everyone can do successfully and are fun and engaging

■ Help children make personal connections

■ Show students their teacher cares about who they are

■ Allow you to get an idea of students' social and academic abilities

Some activity ideas:

■ **Class survey.** Students fill out a survey on favorite school subjects, number of siblings, where they were born, etc. Share the survey results with the class. As a great math activity, graph the survey results.

■ **Class puzzle.** Cut a huge piece of poster board or hefty paper into jigsaw puzzle pieces. Give students a puzzle piece to decorate with their name and pictures of things about themselves. Once everyone has completed a piece, the whole class puts the pieces together. Hang the puzzle in the room or hallway. Its message: Everyone is an important part of our class.

■ **Class scavenger hunt.** Create a scavenger hunt in which students interview each other and find someone who loves soccer, was at a different school in kindergarten, speaks two languages, and so forth. Give students a set amount of time to collect names, then come together to share results.

■ **Wall spaces.** Every student gets part of the classroom wall to use as a personal showcase. (Blue painter's tape makes a great border.) Students bring in or draw pictures of their interests, sports, hobbies, and strengths. The class then walks around examining the wall spaces and collecting information about classmates to share with the whole class.

Sharing

Another component of *Responsive Classroom* Morning Meetings is sharing. Even if you don't do morning meetings, consider setting time aside each day to let students share personal information with each other. A small investment of time in sharing can generate huge rewards. Through sharing, students develop friendships, practice empathy, and come to feel known and comfortable. Sharing also enables them to engage more with school and take more academic risks.

A few possible formats for sharing:

■ **One to three people a day.** Each day, one or a few children share an interest, a hobby, or a story from home. Classmates listen and respond with questions and comments. For example, a sharer might say "This week-end I'm going to my grandmother's house. She's having a birthday, so the whole family will be there." Questioners might ask "How old is your grandmother?" or "Where does she live?" and the sharer responds before the next sharer takes her or his turn.

■ **Around-the-circle.** When many students will want to share at once (such as around holidays and vacations), go around the circle, with each student saying one sentence. The around-the-circle format also works well for sharing academic information or insights. Here's how this might sound:

Teacher: "Today we're each going to share one thing we're excited about in our study of rocks and minerals."

Juan: "I can't wait to go on our field trip to the quarry."

Kristen: "I want to know where gold comes from."

Jamie: "I want to bring in my rock collection."

William: "I'm not sure. I'll pass."

Tory: "I want to learn about volcanoes."

■ **Partners.** Once students have had ample practice with sharing, try having them share with just one partner. This can be especially effective for an academic topic: "Share with your partner how your personal narrative writing is coming along and what you think your next step should be."

■ **Theme share.** Consider occasionally setting aside a bulletin board or special table for sharing about "weekend fun" or "collections." Students can bring pictures or objects for the display and write a sentence or two describing what they brought.

58

Keeping Sharing Safe for Everyone

Sometimes students want to share something that isn't appropriate. Consider this example: *"Last night, my brother was home from college. I walked down into the living room and saw him and his girlfriend on the couch and they were …"* Yikes! We can guess where this might go! This would be a time to jump in: "Hold on, Jordan. Before you tell any more, you can tell the story to me later, and we'll make sure it's okay to share with the class."

Here are some ideas for making sure sharings are safe and appropriate for the whole class.

■ **Brainstorm appropriate topics.** Before students start sharing, have the class brainstorm a list of good topics: pets, friends, trips, hobbies, interests, family events, etc. Hang this list in the circle area for easy reference. You could say to the class "If you think anyone would be embarrassed or upset by something that you're thinking of sharing, you can tell it to me privately first to see if it's okay to share it with the class."

■ **Be sure to use appropriate topics when you model sharing.** Make sure the topics are simple and interesting. Make them the stuff of everyday life, so students see they don't need to impress people with exciting stories.

■ **Preview sharings.** At the beginning of the year, have students quietly tell you their topic ahead of time. This can be a great way to coach them through how to share well while also checking for appropriate content.

■ **Be ready to cut off inappropriate sharings.** When a sharing is beginning to sound inappropriate, quickly and respectfully stop the student. Let the student know that you can chat together about the sharing, if they'd like.

For more information about sharing, see *The Morning Meeting Book*, 3rd ed., by Roxann Kriete and Carol Davis (Center for Responsive Schools, 2014).

No matter what sharing format you use, interactively model and practice first. Teach students how long to share, what is (and isn't) appropriate for sharing in school (see the box "Keeping Sharing Safe for Everyone"), and how to respond to someone else's sharing.

Class Celebrations

It's amazing how a class can come together around a celebration. The end of a unit, other academic accomplishments, and holidays can all inspire class celebrations that foster the group's sense of community and, at the same time, spark or deepen academic learning.

Ideas for Celebrations

The possibilities for community-building and learning-rich celebrations are endless. A few that work well in fourth grade:

- **End of unit.** After finishing a science or social studies unit, have students create a display of their learning by, for example, constructing bulletin boards or setting up tables to show work they've done. Have an open house where students bring in friends and family to see their work.

59

- **Author study.** After spending some time exploring a certain author's books, students set up displays of the books they read and their opinions about the books. Invite families or other classes in to learn about all of the authors. Students can even dress up like a favorite character from one of the books they read.

- **Math celebration.** One year, our class worked really hard on a math unit. On the Friday when we finally finished the unit, we had a math games afternoon. Students could play any game that used math (Monopoly, Sudoku puzzles, Yahtzee, etc.). It was a great way to spend a snowy Friday in February.

(See Chapter 4, "Classroom Games, Special Projects, and Field Trips," for more about special projects similar to these.)

What About Holidays?

Holiday parties can be a source of both great spirits and great contention in schools. Depending on the policies and traditions of your school and district, you may or may not directly celebrate Christmas, Hanukkah, Kwanzaa, Valentine's Day, Halloween, or other holidays. If you do mark these times of the year, be sure the celebrations (1) honor all students' heritages and cultures;

Alternatives to Traditional Celebrations

Occasion	Activity	Curricular Connections
Halloween	**Dress Like a Character.** Students design costumes that depict a favorite character from a book they've read. Best done as an in-class activity so that all students have access to the same resources and needn't depend on family resources for success. On Halloween, students can parade through the school or simply wear their costumes in class. As a bonus, have a special snack that also comes from a favorite read-aloud or class story.	**Reading.** Could connect to lessons on character development, small-group work on particular skills, or a class read-aloud. **Writing.** Students could write a character summary to hang around their necks for the day. **Math.** Measuring and designing costumes can require some complex math skills. **Science/Social Studies.** Students could dress like people they've studied in science and social studies.
Christmas, Hanukkah, Kwanzaa, and other winter holidays	**Solstice Luncheon.** The day of the winter solstice (or as close as you can get), have a class feast. Families can contribute a traditional family dish (from the holiday season or not). The class then sits down to a family-style buffet luncheon where they get to sample dishes from different families and cultures.	**Writing/Social Studies.** Students can do a short write-up of the dish they brought, including where it's from, the main ingredients, and when their family has the dish. **Math.** Encourage families to involve the child in cooking the dish. Cooking provides great real-life application of math skills.
Valentine's Day	**Poetry Pajama Party.** Students come to school in PJs and read poetry to each other or quietly by themselves. Could be the culmination of a poetry-writing unit.	**Reading/Writing.** Poetry slams, partner reading, silent reading, choral reading, reading to reading buddies, and other reading activities can all fit into a day like this.

(2) don't create uncomfortable situations for students whose families don't observe these occasions; and (3) support rather than take attention and time away from the academic and social learning your class is doing. The alternatives to traditional celebrations in the table above meet all three of these goals. (For any celebration involving eating, be sure to check your school or district's policy about bringing homemade food into the classroom.)

Recess

Recess can be a pleasurable time of positive socialization or a time of exclusion, boredom, and inappropriate behavior. If left to themselves, many fourth graders (especially boys) will spend much of their playground time arguing with each other. Many (especially girls) will gather in cliques, which can lead to exclusion and teasing. Whatever the tone and mood, they will transfer to the classroom, affecting children's productivity and spirit of cooperation.

Here are some ways to support fourth grade recess so that students have more fun while building a stronger sense of community.

> **Interactive Modeling**
>
> See Chapter 2, "Schedules and Routines," for a full explanation of Interactive Modeling.

Teach Recess Behavior

We need to teach students playground rules and interactively model and practice expected recess behaviors, even if we don't typically join them for recess. Then we need to hold to these expectations consistently with firm and respectful adult supervision. Investing time, especially at the beginning of school, to teach recess procedures will set children up for success throughout the year.

> **Key Recess Behaviors to Model**
>
> ■ How to use structures (swings, slides, etc.)
>
> ■ Where to get and put away equipment (balls, Hula-hoops, etc.)
>
> ■ How to get an adult's attention
>
> ■ What to do if someone is hurt
>
> ■ How to stay within the play area boundaries
>
> ■ How to respond to the signal for lining up
>
> ■ How to come back into the building
>
> ■ Where to put lunch bags
>
> ■ How to include everyone who wants to join a game
>
> ■ How to ask to join an ongoing game
>
> ■ How to choose sides
>
> ■ How to be a good sport whether your team is winning or losing

Do Structured Recess Sometimes

Although free play is an important part of the school day, there's also a place for structured recess to help students play safely and inclusively. I spend a lot of time playing whole-class recess games at the start of the year as a way to get to know my class and make sure everyone is included in recess games.

Fourth Graders Love Tag!

Here are some variations your class might enjoy:

- **Toilet Tag.** How could fourth graders not love a game named Toilet Tag? People who are tagged kneel or sit with an arm extended (their handle). When someone who is free pushes their handle down, they make a flushing sound and are free to run again.

- **Stuck in the Mud.** Those who are tagged stand still with their feet spread apart. Someone who is free can then free them by crawling between their legs.

- **Category Tag.** When children are about to be tagged, they can avoid being tagged by calling out something from a predetermined category (breakfast foods, U.S. states, math facts that equal 30, etc.). If they don't call something out in time, they're frozen until a free classmate running by releases them with a tap.

Keep tag games safe for everyone:

- **Teach safe tagging.** Use Interactive Modeling to teach and practice how to tag with one open hand on the shoulder. Teach how to avoid the "bathing suit zones." (Any body area that's normally covered by a bathing suit is off limits when tagging.)

- **Start off slowly.** The first tag games can be simple ones (even walking ones) where the goal is to practice safe tagging. As the class is ready, introduce more complex and energetic tag games.

- **Monitor carefully.** Adults should monitor tag games and hold students to high behavior expectations. Reinforce safe tagging: "Wow! You were all taking care of each other with safe tagging. You used gentle touches and tagged each other on the back or the shoulder!" Redirect unsafe tagging: "Micah! Come here for a sec." When he's next to you: "Use an open hand when tagging. You can try again in the next round."

Tips for making structured recess work well:

- **Play tag.** Once you've modeled and practiced recess routines such as safe running and gentle tapping, introduce some simple tag games as a quick way to have good physical fun while practicing those routines. See the box "Fourth Graders Love Tag!" for some good suggestions.

- **Adjust to children's needs.** As the year progresses, adjust how much structured recess you use depending on your students' social needs. Some years, when the social mix is especially challenging, I do some form of structured recess all year long, perhaps one or two days a week. Other years, it may just be a fun once-in-a-while kind of thing. Every year, I'm likely to run some recess games around vacations and as the year winds down, two high-anxiety times of year for students.

Continuous kickball is one good choice for challenging times. In this variation of traditional kickball, there are two teams and there are innings, but no scores and no outs. After the ball is kicked, children run the bases, through home plate and continuing on around, while the fielding team tries to get the ball to home plate as quickly as possible. Once the catcher touches home plate with the ball, students stop running the bases. When the next player kicks, students continue running the bases until the kicked ball reaches home plate. Everyone on the team gets to kick once, and then the teams switch.

Play With Students

If you have the opportunity to go to recess with your class, you'll see that being nearby as children play enables you to supervise them, and refereeing their games allows you to moderate conflicts. But playing with your students when you can gives you the opportunity to model good recess conduct. Students will watch carefully, seeing how you laugh and good-naturedly say, "Darn! You got me!" when you're tagged or how you enjoy the moment while being a good sport when you tag someone else. Don't worry—you don't have to be an athlete to play! The point isn't to demonstrate great physical skill; it's to model friendly and safe playing.

Keep It Quick

If you have an opportunity (other than during scheduled recess) to offer your class a few minutes of active play outside or in the gym, remember that fourth graders exert immense amounts of energy while playing, so they often tire quickly. In ten minutes of playing tag, students will get a good amount of physical release and fresh air and come back energized for more learning. But a twenty-minute running game will likely result in students who can barely keep their heads off their tables when back in the classroom.

63

Lunchtime

Lunch is a built-in time of day for children to hang out with each other, relax, and form bonds. And when lunch is social and relaxing, children come back primed and ready to take on the afternoon's learning challenges. For many children, however, lunch is a time of sitting alone, being teased, or getting into trouble. After such a lunchtime, students will likely reenter the classroom dejected, frustrated, and less able to engage in the social and academic life of the classroom.

You can help set students up for lunchtime success with the following actions.

Key Lunchroom Procedures to Model

- Lining up for food

- Paying or using a ticket system

- Finding a seat

- Responding to the signal for attention

- Using the bathroom

- Throwing away trash

- Lining up for dismissal

- Cleaning tables and floors

- Using an appropriate voice level

Teach Lunchroom Behavior

Even though you may not have lunchtime duty with your students, it's important to teach them the rules of the lunchroom (ideally these will be consistent with the rules of classrooms and other school areas). Start early in the year. Model how to carry out lunchroom procedures in ways that go along with the rules. It's best to do this teaching in the lunchroom, but if this isn't possible, doing it in your own classroom is fine, too. (See Chapter 2, "Schedules and Routines," for more on Interactive Modeling.)

Once you've made your expectations clear and taught the behaviors, hold students to these expectations and correct them respectfully but firmly when they make mistakes. Repeat some of the Interactive Modeling if needed. All this will be time well spent, yielding more peaceful lunches and fewer discipline problems throughout the year.

Assign Seats and Help With Socializing

We've all had the experience of going to a teaching workshop or other large function and having to find a place to eat lunch. We scan the tables, hoping to see someone we know or at least just met. We don't want to eat alone, but neither do we want to intrude on a group. If this sort of thing is hard for us adults, imagine how hard it is for a fourth grader, especially at the beginning of a school year or if the student is new to the school!

To help students socialize successfully at lunch:

■ **To start, assign seats.** At the beginning of the year, assign lunch seats—not just table groups, but actual seats. Put sticky notes with names at lunchroom seats for a few weeks. This eliminates the worry some students feel about finding a seat. It also encourages new friendships. Observe the children (or ask the staff who supervise lunch for their observations) and separate those who tend to be disruptive when seated together.

Sample Fun Facts and Questions

Sample Fun Facts	Sample Fun Questions
Americans eat more than a billion gallons of ice cream each year—enough to fill three Empire State Buildings!	If you could eat only one food for the rest of your life, what would it be? Why?
Fleas can jump 130 times higher than their own height. For humans, this is equal to a six-foot person jumping 780 feet into the air.	If you could choose unlimited life or unlimited money, what would you choose and why?
The world's largest amphibian is the Chinese giant salamander. It can grow up to six feet long.	If you could be a character in any book, who would you be? Why?
The poison arrow frogs of South and Central America are the most poisonous animals in the world.	If you could travel to any place in (or out of) the world, where would you go? What would you do?
Paul Revere never finished his famous ride.	Who's your favorite athlete and why?

■ **Later, vary the seating method.** Some days, have children choose partners to sit with. On other days, do a random drawing of names.

■ **Eat with your students.** If you can, choose one day a week to sit with a group of students for lunch, or join a different group every day for five minutes. The more you get yourself into the lunchroom, the more you can affect its climate and tone.

■ **Promote conversation.** Place conversation starters on lunch tables. Simple questions or facts written on folded cardstock paper can be springboards for conversations. (See "Sample Fun Facts and Questions" above.)

■ **Link to content.** Tie fun facts or questions from the content you're studying into the conversation starters so that students can talk informally about their learning.

■ **Check in.** Follow up after lunch with a brief discussion about the facts and information the class discovered. Doing so sends the message that you care about the children's lunch conversation.

Closing Thoughts

Teachers have multiple opportunities to build a positive community in the classroom. The work and time you invest in building respectful classroom relationships will pay off throughout the year. In fourth grade, children are bursting with new ideas and quickly gaining more mature academic skills. When the classroom community is strong, these strengths can be maximized to make fourth grade a time of explosive growth and immense pleasure for students, and the teaching of fourth graders deeply rewarding for teachers.

CHAPTER 4

Classroom Games, Special Projects, and Field Trips

I recently received an email from a former student. Now in ninth grade, she was looking to reconnect and see how I was doing. She also let me know that she and a couple of friends (also students in that same fourth grade class) had had a sleepover a few days before and they had all decided to watch the movie we created as a class. As a combination literacy/social studies/art project, we had rewritten a read-aloud about the American Revolution into a screenplay, created scenery and costumes, acted it out, and put it all together on a classroom computer. They had a blast watching their copy and said it was their fondest memory of fourth grade.

Children remember special projects like this—along with field trips and favorite class games—long after leaving our classrooms because they gain so much from these experiences. Lively, hands-on ways of learning, along with opportunities to be playful and relaxed at school, actually help children learn academic content more fully. The sheer joy children find in these kinds of learning experiences fosters deep engagement while letting children integrate skills in more complex and challenging ways. Children's sense of community also gets a boost when they share these special, memorable times at school.

And fourth graders are ready for such fun and exciting learning experiences! So many things are coming together for these children: An increase in fine motor ability coincides with an industriousness that makes art and craft projects especially enjoyable. A seriousness about themselves and the world around them primes them for interesting research projects and field trips. That same seriousness makes fourth graders particularly appreciative of fun, relaxing games that let them recharge their energies and connect with their peers in positive ways.

69

Finding Time for Lively Learning

The trick to finding time for engaging, hands-on activities is to embed them into our curricula so they are our work, not an addition to our work. One year, my fourth graders created a class quilt to display their knowledge of geometry. The quilt-making unit lasted for several weeks, with each student contributing one quilt square. The first couple of weeks, students learned about the geometric elements they were to incorporate into their quilt squares—reflections, translations, rotations, and different types of lines and angles. I met with students numerous times as they planned, sketched, and designed their squares. "Show me where a right angle is," I would say to one student. Or, "I see a few different rotations in this design. Which ones do you see?" Then, after we colored the designs with fabric crayons, parents helped to iron the squares onto

fabric and put the whole thing together. The finished quilt hung proudly in our class for the rest of the year.

The project took the same amount of time as the math unit would have, and it was a whole lot more fun and engaging. I believe the students had a deeper understanding of the unit's geometric concepts because of our stimulating and integrated quilt project.

The particular games, projects, and field trips your class does will be shaped by your required curricula, your own interests and talents, the talents and skills colleagues and students' families might contribute—and, of course, your students' needs, interests, and capabilities. Whatever you decide to do with your class, this chapter will give you some guidelines for enlivening learning in ways that are successful and enjoyable for fourth graders.

Classroom Games

There's nothing like a good quick game to energize a class when you see energy levels dipping. Students can laugh together and build community while also stretching their muscles and preparing for more structured learning. The following tips will help you make classroom games successful with fourth graders.

Reduce Competition, Increase Cooperation

Fourth graders' natural tendency to compete, coupled with their tendencies toward anxiety and criticism, can make competitive games frustrating for them. For example, I remember once playing a game of Jeopardy with the class to wrap up a science unit on the solar system. I was hoping students would enjoy the playfulness of the game while we reviewed a lot of information that was coming up on a test the next day. But because there were

points attached to the game and only one team could win, students began turning on teammates with angry voices when someone made a mistake. I had to end the game early because the tone of the classroom was getting worse and worse. The next year, I came up with a new game to play that didn't put one student on the spot to win or lose points for their team, and the tone was much more positive.

Wherever possible, take the competition out of class games. If you want some competition, consider having the class compete as a team to beat the clock or their own record.

Two suggestions for noncompetitive games:

- **Group juggling.** How many juggling balls can you keep in the air at once? Establish a pattern where everyone tosses a juggling ball (or stuffed animal or bean bag) to another in the circle until everyone has taken a turn. Keep the ball moving through that pattern, and gradually add more balls until the game collapses. Record how many balls you had going, and try to break your class record next time you play.

- **Class scavenger hunt.** How many right angles can the class find in the classroom in three minutes? Record the class results on a chart and play again the next day to see if they can beat their record.

Keep It Light and Fun

Fourth graders can be so serious! We can ease that seriousness by keeping the tone of games light and relaxed. When playing a whole-class game of Boggle, for example, emphasize that it's okay if some people find more words than others . . . that's just how the game goes. When playing games with the class, demonstrate yourself how to lose gracefully, laughing as another student hits a home run in baseball multiplication against you!

71

Keep It Quick

Whether outside or in the gym, fourth graders tend to play hard, so they often tire quickly. If you're playing a game of predator tag to reinforce the idea of a food web, it would be better to play for ten minutes than twenty. If a running game goes too long, students will collapse into exhausted sweaty heaps back in the classroom, unable to refocus on the next learning task.

Move Throughout the Day

In the classroom, quick movement breaks throughout the day add an element of playfulness and refuel children's brains for more learning. Try a three-minute round of "Simon Says" or "Heads, Shoulders, Knees, and Toes" between spelling and writing. You'll find these quick activities will also keep you lively and engaged for better teaching.

Provide an Appropriate Amount of Challenge

Fourth graders love challenge, but too much challenge can overwhelm them. The key is finding activities that provide some opportunities for scaffolding, improvement, or individual choice and challenge. For example, group juggling is often really hard for a class at first. I once had a class that could keep only three balls going to start with, but by the end of the year, they could handle twelve!

72

Learn More About Classroom Games

99 Activities and Greetings: Great for Morning Meeting . . . and other meetings, too! by Melissa Correa-Connolly (Center for Responsive Schools, 2004).

Energizers! 88 Quick Movement Activities That Refresh and Refocus by Susan Lattanzi Roser (Center for Responsive Schools, 2009).

The Morning Meeting Book, 3rd ed., by Roxann Kriete and Carol Davis (Center for Responsive Schools, 2014).

Other activities that provide fun, safe challenges for fourth graders:

■ **Twenty Questions.** Fourth graders love to use logic and reasoning to solve problems. Begin with a relatively simple object to guess (such as "cat") and choose more challenging objects as the class gets better (such as "oak leaf"). This game is also great for use in your academic curriculum. For example, if you're studying the solar system, you could have students try to guess "asteroid belt."

- **"Challenge yourself" math problem.** Have everyone create and solve a math problem that relates to the day's math lesson. This way, all students get to create their own level of challenge.

- **Complex chants and songs.** Fourth graders enjoy language play. Teach your class chants and songs; for ideas, see "Movement, Games, Songs, and Chants" in the resource list at the end of this book. Chances are some of your students know some great chants and songs, too. Have them teach these to the class—after they check with you to make sure that what they'd like to teach is appropriate.

Special Projects

Think back to your own elementary school experience. What schoolwork do you most clearly remember? I remember a class play, a huge painting project, and making a holiday wreath out of pine cones, acorns, and wire. These kinds of projects stuck with me because they were fun, challenging, and deeply engaging.

Class projects for which students use a variety of skills, talents, and media can be some of the most rewarding and exciting parts of the school year. Such projects do require planning and preparation, but they're definitely worth the effort.

The following suggestions will help keep projects doable for fourth graders—and for you.

Keep Groups Small

Fourth graders tend to be more comfortable and successful when working in pairs, rather than groups. Two fourth graders working together can usually negotiate the details of how to divvy up the work—how to share the fact-gathering for a poster, who does the artwork, and who writes the text. If you must create groups of four or five, clearly delineate different roles for students within the group.

Sample Project Checklist

Research Project Tasks	✓ When Complete
Choose topic.	
Generate list of questions (at least 10).	
Collect first 20 facts.	
Have peer conference.	
Collect next 20 facts.	
Have teacher conference.	
Organize facts using color coding.	
Generate list of projects.	
Have peer conference.	
Plan/sketch projects.	
Have teacher conference.	
Create projects.	
Plan presentation.	
Have teacher conference.	
Present projects and facts to class.	
Fill out a self-evaluation.	

74

Try Some Individual Projects

One year, each student studied an animal living in New Hampshire—our state. We took a field trip to a science center to observe animals up close, and each student created a model of an animal in papier-mâché. Students worked together as they looked through books, took notes, colored posters, and painted their models, but each student had control of his or her own project and got to be the expert on a particular animal.

Keep Large Projects Bite-Sized

Fourth graders are incredibly industrious and get really excited about taking on a huge project (a class movie, say, or a class hike and camp-out). But without the proper scaffolding and structure, they'll quickly get overwhelmed and give up. Help students keep the work manageable by breaking large tasks into a series of smaller tasks so they can feel the accomplishment of completing each part of the project. Checklists of mini-tasks, with due dates for each, help students manage their work.

Use Gentle Assessments

Fourth graders can be particularly sensitive to what they see as criticism and may worry that you'll use impersonal letter grades or critical feedback to assess their work. Focus your assessments, especially of finished work, on the positives. Offer constructive suggestions during work periods, when students have a chance to improve their work before it's finished.

Assessing Fourth Graders	
Suggested Assessments	**Assessments to Avoid**
■ **Checklists.** Students can simply check off project requirements as they complete them.	■ **Peer assessments.** Fourth graders can often be critical of others. Having them assess others' work can lead to overly harsh assessments.
■ **Rubrics.** Students can help create their own rubrics for what qualities or elements should be in their final projects.	■ **Letter grades.** Impersonal and often subjective, letter grades used in isolation give little information that students can use to improve their work.
■ **Self-assessments.** Teach students how to honestly appraise their own work (focusing on positives).	■ **One-word feedback.** Words such as "Great!" or "Sloppy" give children little to go on. Instead, offer specific assessments that reinforce the good and offer suggestions for growth.
■ **Lists.** Bulleted lists of "things done well," coupled with one or two "suggestions for next time" can help encourage thoughtful reflection.	■ **√+, √, √–.** Like letter grades, check marks tend to be too general to offer valuable feedback.
■ **Narratives.** Writing a simple note or letter highlighting what a student did well and giving one or two ideas for improvement personalizes your feedback.	■ **Public assessment.** Students should not be assessed in front of others. Once they have done a presentation or shared their work, a private conference or paper-based assessment is more appropriate.

Give Choices

All students, perhaps especially fourth graders, engage more with school when they have choices about their learning, so give students some power and control over their learning whenever practical. For example, you might offer three different books about state history and require all students to read at least one as part of their state research. While learning about outer space in science, students might get to choose between creating a Power-Point presentation, constructing a 3-D model, or putting on a short play to demonstrate what they've learned to the class.

Field Trips

Field trips can be fantastic ways to study science and social studies content in a personal and exciting way. A trip to a local textile mill to study a historically significant state industry can help bring history alive for fourth graders. Visiting a wildlife center can give students hands-on experiences with animals and conversations with scientists that ignite their curiosity, making classroom follow-up work more meaningful. For many students, field trips also offer opportunities their parents may be unable to provide.

Given the somewhat anxious mood of many fourth graders, it's vital to set students up for success. Here are some tips.

Keep Groups Small

Small groups, which make sense for lots of work with fourth graders, are crucial for successful field trips. Even if you must have larger groups for logistical reasons (such as chaperone coverage), you can partner students within their bigger groups. Knowing with whom they'll be eating lunch, riding on the bus, and touring the site reduces students' worries and eliminates arguments.

Consider Same-Gender Groups

Normally, I mix boys and girls together throughout the day because it's important for fourth graders to practice working with everyone, even though boys often prefer working with boys and girls prefer other girls. I've found, however, that it's best not to push this point on field trips.

Most fourth graders will feel safer and more relaxed if they can be with classmates of their choosing (or at least be with a partner of their choosing within a mixed group).

Make the Schedule and Expectations Clear Ahead of Time

As the excitement (and anxiety) builds in the days leading up to the field trip, you'll be bombarded with questions: "Where are we going?" "What are we going to do?" "When does the bus leave?" "Where will the bathrooms be?"

Not only will the children be full of questions, but they'll ask the same questions over and over. Reminding yourself what these questions are really about can help you avoid frustration: "These kids are worried. They need to hear information many times to feel reassured."

Ways for students to keep hold of the information they need:

■ **Information card.** Give each child a card-stock copy of the day's important information (schedule, partners, what to bring, etc.). Have extra copies on hand for students who lose theirs.

■ **Question time.** Give students a few minutes each day (right before they head home) to write down their questions on sticky notes. Post the questions on a chart and answer them at various times throughout the next day.

■ **Quick class meetings.** Schedule several meetings to discuss how classroom rules will work on the field trip. Get specific: "How will we 'Be Safe' while riding the bus?" "How will we 'Be Respectful' when listening to a speaker?"

Make the Field Trip Appropriate for Fourth Graders

Imagine yourself with a fourth grade class at a stone quarry. This should be a great chance to do some hands-on work identifying and classifying rocks and minerals. Students sit on large boulders in the hot sun as a guide begins explaining the difference between sedimentary, igneous, and metamorphic rocks. For the first five minutes, the children sit still, eyes glued on the speaker. But the speaker goes on—and on. By the thirty-minute mark, you're quietly praying for the ordeal to end as you spend all your energy subtly trying to get children who are wiggling, slouching, or looking into the woods to sit upright and pay attention.

To avoid such scenarios, make sure you know what's planned for your students at your field trip site. How long will a speaker address the group? (Aim for no more than ten minutes at a time.) Will students spend a lot of time actively exploring the area? (Our stone quarry guide would have been more effective if he'd given a five-minute explanation of the rock types and then sent students off on a scavenger hunt to find examples of each.)

If there will be no guide or instructor, make sure your fourth graders will be able to read and take notes from the information available. If possible, visit the site yourself beforehand so you'll know just what to expect.

Think About Lunch and Restroom Needs

Before you go, sharing with the children details about when and where they'll have lunch and where the bathrooms will be will help them feel secure.

■ **Bringing or buying lunch.** How will lunch work for students who normally get school lunches in the lunchroom? Schools will often provide bag lunches for field trips, but it's best to check about this early on and let students know how it will work.

■ **Drinks.** Make sure to communicate to parents and students what kinds of drinks are (and aren't) acceptable. Usually, glass bottles and sodas are not allowed on field trips. What should students bring? Will there be a cooler to keep milk cold? Will there be a water fountain or other source of water for students who need it?

■ **Food allergies.** If parents are packing their child's lunch or snack for the field trip, make sure to tell them (and students) if regular allergy policies apply—for example, no foods containing peanuts, no swapping lunches. Also, check to see if your school follows different food rules on field trips. Extra precautions might be needed when multiple classes are traveling together, mixing children with different food allergies.

■ **Eating arrangements.** Let students know where they'll be eating and how seating arrangements will work. Will students eat inside or outside? Will there be tables or benches or will they sit on the floor somewhere? If students will need to eat at tables, it can save a lot of anxiety to announce seat assignments early on.

■ **Bathrooms.** Where will students be able to use bathrooms? Consider having students buddy up for bathroom use so they have someone to go in with. This can help alleviate some worries about using a strange facility. Also, make sure students know whom they should tell when they need to use a bathroom so you (or chaperones) always know where students are. Be sure to remind students to use the bathrooms before long bus rides to reduce the chance of having to look for a stopping place along the way!

Plan Downtime

Planning lots of downtime for snacks, bathroom breaks, running games, and quiet time will give students the energy they need to follow the rules and to learn. Bring along your class read-aloud so that students can settle in and rest after lunch and recess.

Give Structured Learning Tasks

If left to roam and wander aimlessly on a field trip, fourth graders will . . . roam and wander aimlessly. On one class nature walk, I asked students to write and sketch in their nature journals as we walked. When we got back to school, few students had written or drawn anything! On a similar trip the next year, I gave each student a checklist of things to observe and record (find something that hibernates, a plant that doesn't have chlorophyll, an animal that's both predator and prey). With more structure, students were much more productive.

Checklists, scavenger hunts, worksheets, and other such tools can tap into fourth graders' sense of industry and curiosity. You'll be amazed at how many facts a group can gather when given the right challenge, guidance, and structure.

Anticipate Behavior Changes

Student behavior usually changes on field trips. Someone who is normally quiet and reserved becomes bouncy and boisterous. A student who needs constant management in the classroom suddenly becomes a model rule-follower, appearing nervous or even sad. Students who typically ask tons of questions clam up during Q&A sessions with guest speakers.

Just knowing that students will act differently can get us in a good mind-set for managing these new behaviors. Often, what we need to do is similar to what we'd do to maintain good classroom discipline: Be consistent. Be fair. Be clear. Follow through. Be patient. Many times, these different behaviors can just be ignored (baby talk on the bus doesn't hurt anyone). If it can't be ignored (baby talk while asking a guide a question is a problem), use a calm demeanor and redirect the behavior: "Use your regular voice."

Also, make sure to use the same kinds of procedures and signals that you use in the classroom so that children understand that the field trip is still part of school. For example, use the same signal for quiet (whether it's a raised hand, a chime, or another signal you always use) and have students raise their hand to ask a question when you meet as a group.

Plan the Transition Back to School

Consider ways to help students transition back to the classroom or safely off to parents at the end of a field trip. I remember once just telling students to get off the bus and meet me in the classroom. The ensuing scene brought to mind college kids rushing the court at the conclusion of a championship basketball game. Students ran through the halls, high-fiving other students, shouting, dropping backpacks, and causing general mayhem and chaos.

To help fourth graders transition back to school:

- **Remind students about rules and routines.** Before students head back into the building, help them get back into "school mode." Remind everyone of how we walk in the hallways. Make sure students know what to do when they reenter the classroom. What should they do with their backpacks? Should they sit in their seats or meet in the circle?

- **Let students know what's next.** Remember, fourth graders love to know what's coming next, so let students know what you'll be doing after you're in the room. If students were collecting notes or had school supplies that need to be organized, let them know how to put these things away. (I'll never forget the time I didn't do this. The next day, I asked students to turn in notes and several students had thrown them away, not realizing they would need them later on!)

- **Give a task for the walk back.** You might pair students up and have them whisper with each other on the way back to the room. "Choose the three best things you saw today. Be ready to share with others." Or you might have students think quietly about the most important thing they learned.

- **Have chaperones help.** If you have chaperones, have one lead the class down the hall, or have students get into small groups and have each group walk with a chaperone. This adult presence can help the children stay calm and ease the transition back to the classroom.

Closing Thoughts

The sense of playfulness that classroom games, special projects, and field trips inject into the school day can be especially helpful for fourth graders, with their tendency to be so serious. By working these opportunities into the curriculum, we give children fun opportunities to integrate skills and practice collaboration. Most important, though, these lively ways of learning lead to deep engagement, which helps keep children passionate about learning while enhancing their academic achievement.

CHAPTER 5

Communicating With Parents

My first year teaching fourth grade was also my first year teaching, and I had an opportunity to test my skills of parent communication right off the bat. About one month into the year, my principal called me into her office to let me know that a parent wanted to switch his daughter out of my class. "Good grief!" I thought. "What did I do?" It turns out that this student's brother (who was ten months older) was in a class across the hall, and he was coming home with math worksheets, reading assignments in a science textbook, and other homework assignments every night. I hadn't been giving nearly as much homework, and the parent felt that I wasn't challenging his daughter enough. He added that his daughter had had a first-year teacher the year before, and he felt that it wasn't fair for her to have two first-year teachers in a row.

I talked to my principal and let her know that I wanted to try meeting with this father to hear his concerns directly and try to open a dialogue with him. He came in one day after school that week, and I spent time showing him around the classroom, explaining our spelling program, showing him his daughter's reading journal and writing notebook, and talking about the challenging science projects we had just started. He left satisfied and agreed to leave his daughter in my class. While I felt relieved, I decided from that day on that I would communicate more effectively with all parents about my teaching approach and the reasoning behind it so that parents wouldn't be left confused or concerned.

83

About the Term "Parent"

Students come from a variety of homes with a variety of family structures. Many children are being raised by grandparents, siblings, aunts and uncles, and foster families. All of these people are to be honored for devoting their time, attention, and love to raising children. Coming up with one word that encompasses all these caregivers is challenging. For simplicity's sake, this chapter uses the word "parent" to refer to anyone who is the child's primary caregiver.

Like all parents, fourth grade parents need to know how you'll be guiding their child's growth at school. Sharing this information early and often helps alleviate worries that parents may have while enabling them to support their child's learning and enjoy the particular strengths of fourth graders. Don't worry, you don't have to meet with each parent one-on-one after school— the dad who wanted to pull his daughter out of my class was unusual—but you do need to get information flowing to and from parents early on and stay in good communication throughout the year.

In this chapter, we'll look at key communication strategies and consider ways to respond to specific concerns of fourth grade parents.

Strategies for Good Communication

Start Reaching Out Early

Communicate early—before the school year starts if you've received your class list—with positive information about your classroom. This sets the tone for the year. If your first contact with parents is about a problem at school, that interaction will set the tone for the year. With a positive first contact, if a problem comes up later, solving it with parents will go more smoothly.

A few ways to set a positive tone right from the start:

- **Friendly letter.** Introduce yourself and let parents know you're excited about the upcoming year. Briefly explain what fourth grade will be like, and tell parents how and when they can contact you.

- **Informal classroom visit.** As the summer draws to a close, invite families in to see your classroom. Make it a day when you were going to be setting up for the year anyway, and a time when working parents will likely be available. The visit will help ease your new students' fears, and that will help their parents relax, too.

- **Call or note home.** During the first couple of weeks of school, make a phone call or send a note or email message to every child's home to say something positive about the beginning of their year. ("Alexis has had a great first week. She's already written a couple of pages in her writing journal!")

Sample Letter to Parents

Dear Parents and Caregivers,

Welcome to fourth grade! I am really looking forward to our upcoming year together. Fourth grade is an exciting year for students and parents, and I'd like to give you a little information about the beginning of the year.

First, let me introduce myself briefly. I have been teaching for fifteen years in third, fourth, and fifth grades. I've been here at our school since 1999. When I'm not in school, I love to spend time with my wife, Heather, and two children, Ethan and Carly. I also love to garden and swim.

This year our class will be exploring a lot of exciting topics. In science we will learn about geology, the solar system, electricity, and nutrition. In social studies we will learn a lot about New Hampshire, both its history and what is going on currently. In math we're going to dive into geometry, multi-digit multiplication, and division. In literacy, we'll be having reading workshop and writing workshop. We've got some fun units in poetry, report writing, and an author study on the way this fall!

As the year begins, we will spend some time learning the routines of the class and getting to know each other. As we explore new learning topics and review some content from third grade, we will also work at becoming a strong community together. When students feel safe and comfortable in their classrooms, they are better able to take on academic challenges.

In a few weeks, we will have our annual Back to School Night. Here's something you can start thinking about for that evening: What are your hopes for your fourth grader this year in school? What kinds of academic and social goals do you have for your child? I look forward to talking with you about that.

Please contact me if you have any questions. You can email me at mr_anderson@school.org or call me at home anytime before 8:00 PM (XXX-XXX-XXXX). I look forward to meeting you and to a great year!

■ **Formal open house ("Back to School Night").** Most schools have an open house within the first month or two of the school year. Use this as a chance to continue making positive connections. Highlight exciting things happening in the classroom, give parents a chance to see the kinds of work that the class will be doing, and let parents know how they can support their children in school. Open house is also a good time to share a little information about typical developmental characteristics of fourth graders. (See "Share Information about Child Development" on the next page.)

Emailing Parents

In general, serious or confidential matters are best discussed in person, by phone, or in a paper-and-envelope letter. But email can be great for quick notes about day-to-day classroom life. A few things to consider:

■ **Know if parents can—and want to—use email.** At the fall open house, invite parents to sign up to receive email from you if they'd like. Tell them you'll also be communicating in other ways. Judge by the number of signups whether to use email regularly.

■ **Keep the volume of messages manageable by mixing in other ways of communicating.** Most parents rely less on email once they know you'll be sharing news in various ways.

■ **Follow the guidelines.** Check whether your school, district, or parent organization has guidelines for emailing families.

Do Parents Have Language or Literacy Issues?

Be on the lookout for indications that students' parents have difficulty reading. If they do, be careful about relying on written information too often. Look for other ways to communicate, such as phone calls or recorded messages that parents can call in to receive.

■ **Website.** If your school has a website with a page for each teacher, you may choose to use it as a place to post general information about classroom happenings.

Listen

Parents are experts on their own children and can give you many valuable insights that will help you teach their child. Parents can also give you information about the family that's relevant to the child's school life. Whenever you communicate with parents, make it a two-way street by inviting them to share their thoughts and insights.

Empathize

It hurts when your child hurts. All parents want to do whatever they can to help their child succeed in school, so it's natural for parents to be stressed out when their child is feeling anxious about a science project or hurt because of a friendship struggle. If you're dealing with an angry parent, keep in mind that often parents experience fear, but express it as anger. When we think of our goal as to ease a parent's fear, we're likely to be supportive, focusing on positive solutions instead of getting defensive and angry ourselves.

I remember once having a parent on the phone, furious because I wasn't being tough enough on her son for misspelling words in daily assignments. (She wanted me to circle them all in red pen and require her son to practice them.) As we talked, I realized that she was scared that her son wasn't a good enough speller. Instead of giving in to my initial inclination to defend my approach to teaching spelling, I invited her in for a conference. I showed her some samples of her son's writing and assured her that he was just where he was supposed to be as a fourth grader. This opened up communication between us and helped ease her fears.

Communicate Regularly and Consistently

Parents generally appreciate being "in the loop" and are more likely to feel like partners in their child's education if they're regularly informed about the goings-on of the classroom. Keep the information you send brief, focused, and positive. Good topics are classroom activities and accomplishments, upcoming special projects or events, and developmental changes they might see in their child during fourth grade.

Whether you send out a weekly email update, post to a webpage (find out your school's or district's guidelines for this), send letters home with students, or guide students in recording the week's highlights in a class newsletter, try to follow a consistent schedule and format. Parents are more likely to review and respond to your communications if they know what to expect and when to expect it.

Share Information About Child Development

It can be confusing for parents to see their child changing, even if these changes are common ones in children. So the more you communicate with them about the often-seen characteristics and changes in fourth graders, the better.

One way to do this is to send home a chart of typical characteristics. I like to give parents copies of child development pamphlets based on the book *Yardsticks: Child and Adolescent Development Ages 4–14* by Chip Wood (Center for Responsive Schools, 2018). At formal open houses and parent-teacher conferences, we look at the pamphlets together, and I highlight the changes that their child is experiencing or might experience as the year rolls on.

Key points to make as you talk with families about their fourth grader's development:

- **Rates of growth differ among children.** Human growth and development is complex, and no two children reach a particular milestone at the same time. Fourth graders, for example, are usually ready to master cursive writing, but some will do so earlier in the year and some later.

- **Physical, cognitive, and social growth rates may differ.** For example, a child may build reading skills rapidly but need more time to get the hang of working with peers, a physically gifted child may need extra supports to learn math, and so on.

- **Children will change as the year progresses.** In fourth grade, a child may begin the year loving to play with many friends (typical of many third graders) but by the middle or end of the year struggle with friendship groups and prefer one friend at a time (typical of many fourth graders).

- **Growth often happens in fits and starts.** Children may go through an explosive period of growth followed by a lag or even a regression.

Child Development Resources for Parents

Yardsticks: Child and Adolescent Development Ages 4–14 by Chip Wood (Center for Responsive Schools, 2018), or the child development pamphlets based on this book.

- **Fourth graders have tremendous energy, but tire quickly.** Their energy can be a great asset in the classroom, giving them stamina for large projects and exciting work increases. But it's also normal for them to come home from school exhausted. It's okay for them to take breaks while doing homework.

- **Fourth graders can be emotionally sensitive.** Encouragement and patience from adults can boost their confidence, while sarcasm and exasperation can be crushing.

Let Parents Know How They Can Help

All parents want their children to succeed. But fourth graders often pull away when parents try to talk with them about school. You can help by letting parents know what they can do to help their child. Remind them about the importance of healthy food and good sleep. Early in the year, survey parents' interests and skills and invite them to share their talents in special classroom activities. (For more on having parents in the classroom, see "Involving Parents in Events and Activities" on page 96.)

Special Concerns of Fourth Grade Parents

Some parental concerns take on special meaning in fourth grade. Here are some of the most common concerns, along with suggestions for how to respond.

How Does My Child Compare With the Rest of the Class?

This is a question at every grade, but in fourth grade it may take on more urgency. Standardized tests become more frequent and more involved. Middle school looms. Hypercompetitive fourth graders may worry that they don't measure up. Spelling lists and math facts sent home for practice can become fodder for power struggles and tears.

But at every grade, parents' underlying concern is the same: "Is my child doing okay?" Address that concern honestly and calmly, without comparing the child with classmates. Instead, focus on the child's own strengths and

Talking With Parents:
Sample Responses to Two Common Questions

"How does my child compare with classmates?"

- "Antoine is doing really well in reading. He's currently working on a challenging book, and he's handling it well. Here's a sample of his reading journal that shows some of his best thinking."

- "Lisa's spelling is about what I expect to see in fourth grade. Let's look at the spelling in this sample of her writing. She made a few really common mistakes. *Because*, *people*, and *girls* are all tough words for fourth graders. When we count up the correct words, we find that she spelled ninety-two precent of the words correctly. That's just fine."

- "Mark struggled with our last math unit. He understood this first objective about drawing fractions, but he didn't understand these next few about equivalency and adding fractions. I'd like to do some extra work with him for a couple of days to help him out. Let's talk about possible ways we can do this."

"How are you going to challenge my child?"

- "Social studies is a rich experience in fourth grade. The children will put together multifaceted research projects incorporating reading, writing, note taking, art, problem-solving, and oral presentation skills. They're going to learn a lot!"

- "In science this year, we'll explore several complex topics, including astronomy, geology, and biology. Each student will learn how to perform scientific observations and conduct scientific experiments."

- "I know that spelling is often a hot-button issue in fourth grade. Because students all have different strengths and challenges as spellers, I'll work with each of them individually during writing conferences to help them grow in this skill."

challenges. Talk about the child's progress in relation to the goals that have been set for him or her and the established standards for fourth graders. Be as specific as possible. (See the "Talking With Parents" chart on the opposite page.)

How Are You Going to Challenge My Child?

Many parents report that when they ask their fourth grader "How's school going?" the child answers, "I'm bored." It's understandable that when parents hear this response, they'll want to ask you to challenge their child more. Help parents understand that "I'm bored in school" from a fourth grader often means "I don't understand something," "I'm worried about something," or "I don't really feel like talking about school right now."

Encourage parents to try more specific questions such as "What did you work on in math today?" "What are you studying in science right now?" and "What's your favorite thing about school right now?" Information from your webpage or the update letters you send home can also help parents come up with specific questions about their child's current schoolwork.

Even if they understand the "I'm bored" code-speak, however, many parents will still be concerned about challenge in fourth grade. Try working specifics about how you'll challenge children into your routine communications with parents, and send a message loud and clear at open house night that students will be challenged in fourth grade. (See the "Talking With Parents" chart.)

What Will Homework Be Like This Year?

Both teachers and parents struggle with homework. Some see homework as a way to practice skills and build responsibility. Others worry that homework wastes children's time and energy.

As children enter fourth grade, the homework question may become particularly worrisome. Fourth grade is typically the year when the amount of homework begins to increase. It's also the year when children are more likely to resist homework and to struggle with it.

A few tips for nurturing student and family success with homework:

■ **Assign purposeful homework that's appropriate for fourth graders.** Make sure homework has a clear, learning-related purpose. Also, be sure each assignment offers practice in already-learned skills so that students can truly do their homework independently. Finally, design assignments that don't require too much time—especially important with fourth graders, who are often very tired by the end of the school day.

■ **Teach homework skills at school.** At the beginning of the year, I have students do their homework assignments at school so I can teach homework skills and observe students' ability to work independently. Do they, for example, know how to choose a place where they can work with minimal distraction? Read through the assignment to make sure they understand what they need to do? Gather any necessary supplies before they begin to work? Only when I'm sure students can handle homework on their own do I assign "at home" homework.

■ **Make sure students take responsibility.** I actually told parents at an open house one year that they were not allowed to have power struggles with their fourth graders over homework. I was the one assigning the work, so I would be the one to hold the children accountable if they didn't do it. I explained that parents could certainly ask about homework, check in on it, and remind students to do it, but if students refused or started to engage them in a power struggle, parents had my permission to disengage and let me handle things at school. Parents actually stood up and applauded.

■ **Give students ways to get help.** I give students my home phone number and hours when they can call me if they need help. You could also have each student exchange phone numbers with a classmate so they can call each other with homework questions. (Before giving out or exchanging phone numbers—including your own—check school policy to make sure it's okay to do so.) Or you might have students review (and even start) their homework in the last few minutes before they leave school to make sure they know what to do.

- ■ **Periodically update parents.** For example, give them the percentage of homework their child has turned in on time. Every Friday, send completed homework home in a folder with a comment sheet for parents to review and sign.

- ■ **Be realistic.** Some of your students may live in conditions that make doing homework very challenging or even impossible; some students may be homeless. Be ready to modify and adjust homework expectations accordingly.

Why Is My Child Having More Friend Problems This Year?

Social problems are a common concern for fourth graders, especially girls. Watch third graders at recess, and you'll likely see large groups of children moving in packs, playing games of imagination while running and shouting together. Fourth grade recess often looks more subdued, with pairs and trios of students (again, especially girls) walking and talking.

Even though these changes are common, it's still painful for parents when their children are struggling with friendship issues. Reassuring parents that this is a typical shift can be comforting, but it's also nice to offer suggestions. For example, you might know that two children have interests in common. You could suggest that parents encourage the friendship outside of school, if both children are interested.

At the same time, observe the child (during recess, if necessary) to make sure there isn't something more to the parents' worries. If you see signs of more serious social problems that do not seem to be resolving over time, talk to your school or district guidance counselor, psychologist, or social worker for advice on next steps.

Holding Productive Parent–Teacher Conferences

Parent–teacher conferences are great opportunities to deepen your positive relationship with parents, resolve concerns about their child, and share insights about child development. Here are a few things you can do to make these conferences go smoothly.

Offer Conversation Starters

To put parents at ease and get the conversation flowing, have some questions ready: "What did your child like about school last year?" "What does she like to do at home?" "What are some of your goals for your child this year?"

If appropriate for the parents of your students, you might want to send these questions home in written form at the start of the year, rather than asking in person. Then both you and the parents will have time to think about the questions and possible responses.

Invite Parents to Share Their Thoughts

We teachers often have so much we want to say at conferences that we forget to listen to what parents have to say. But as experts on their child, they have valuable insights. "Please tell me your thoughts" or "What have you been noticing?" are simple ways to signal that you're ready to hear what they have to say.

Highlight the Positives

Even struggling students have positive qualities. Warmly recognize a child's strengths before launching into a discussion of her struggles. This gives parents some perspective and encourages them to work productively with you. You might say, for example, "Cate has complex, unique ideas about our readings and our projects" before getting into how Cate needs to work on being patient with classmates who can't keep up with her ideas.

Tackle Only One or Two Issues

If you list too many problems, parents (and children) are likely to feel defeated. Instead, you can mention that there are several things you'd like to work on with the child, but that for now you're going to concentrate on just the one or two challenges that are the best next steps for the student to work on. Later, when other issues need to be addressed, use the same strategy. "Your son has grown in some really positive ways over the past few weeks. His writing is becoming more developed, his homework has been coming in more regularly, and he has been much calmer at the end of the day! So our next step is to help him with a friendship challenge he's having right now."

Be Prepared to Handle Surprises

Sometimes, parents surprise us with a negative or personal question or comment: "Last year, my son's teacher bullied him all year. She used to scream at him if he forgot to write his name on his paper!" "My daughter is so lazy. She never tries at anything." "My husband doesn't care about Darren. He never comes to these conferences."

When this happens, we don't want to be dismissive, but neither do we want to betray the trust of a colleague or try to counsel a parent about personal issues. Some strategies to try if something like this comes up:

- **Listen with empathy.** "That must have been hard" or "You've been through a lot" can let a parent know she or he has been heard without offering our own opinion or advice.

- **Offer to get help.** "It sounds like you're wondering what to do next. Our school counselor may have some ideas of what to try."

- **Stay focused on the child.** If a parent is talking about his or her personal problems, not about the child, try and move the conversation back to the student. "It sounds like you are all going through some tough stuff right now. I wonder if that's taking Stefan's focus away from math. Do you have some ideas about how we could help him concentrate?"

- **Take some thinking time.** When faced with a really difficult question, it's fine to let the parent know that you need some time to think and observe. "Wow. I didn't realize that Sherry had such a tough year last year. I'm going to do some research in our files and observe Sherry closely for a few days. Then I'll get back to you." Be sure to follow up and let the parents know what you discovered and how you think you might address the issue.

Sample Guidelines for Parent Volunteers

Thanks for volunteering in our classroom!
Here are some guidelines and some information to help you out:

Class Routines

- **Hand signal/chime.** When I raise my hand or ring the chime, that's our class signal to stop working and look at me. Adults can help by doing the same.

- **Bathroom sign-out.** Students may sign out to use the bathroom on their own. They can help explain our process if you have questions.

Volunteer Guidelines

- **Adult voice.** Adult voices can sometimes carry farther than we think. When working with a student (or a small group), make sure to use a quiet voice so others can stay focused on their work.

- **Discipline.** If a student is refusing to do work or being at all disruptive, let me know, and I will handle the situation.

- **Privacy.** As a volunteer in our classroom, you may see a student having a hard time. Please respect the privacy of all students by not discussing the issue outside of our classroom.

- **Anything else.** If you have any questions at all, please come let me know.

Involving Parents in Events and Activities

Inviting parents into the classroom lets them experience some of their child's school life. It also gains you some help for projects that are hard to manage by yourself. The following tips will help make these parent volunteer times productive and enjoyable for everyone.

Set Expectations for Parents

To succeed in your classroom, parents need to know what you expect of them. When visiting adults break rules—for example, by using inappropriate language or talking while you're giving directions—the children may become confused or anxious. Prevent this problem by sending home or passing out simple written guidelines for visitors (see sample on page 96). You could also review the rules orally as students and adult visitors listen together.

Maintain Consistent Discipline

Children often behave differently when their families come to school. Don't be surprised to see fourth graders pushing limits, using baby talk, or reverting to other younger behaviors. Let children know that classroom rules still apply when their parents are visiting, and be ready to discipline firmly and kindly.

Here are behaviors you might see and ways you could respond.

When Children Misbehave During Family Visits	
Situation	**What You Might Say or Do**
Billy's father is ironing leaves onto wax paper for a nature collage. Billy is giggling and slapping his dad's leg, clearly happy to have his dad in the room but unsure of how to interact with his dad in this setting. Billy's dad is ignoring the behavior but is clearly uncomfortable.	"Billy, your dad has a job to do right now. Come sit with me for a few minutes so he can do it, and then you can try again to work with your group."
Maria is usually a mature fourth grader, but when her mother comes in for a morning meeting, Maria uses baby talk and tries to sit in her lap.	"Maria, use a regular voice. You can sit next to your mom or you can sit in a different spot if that's better for you."
Michael is a rule-follower. He raises his hand to speak and keeps his hands to himself. But when his uncle chaperones a field trip, Michael becomes aggressive, pushing other students.	"Michael, our class rules say that we need to be safe. Come sit with me for a bit. You can rejoin your group when you're calm and ready to be safe."

Keep Groups Small

Fourth graders tend to work better in pairs than in groups of four or five, and parents may have their hands full if a fairness issue erupts among five anxious fourth graders. Keeping groups small will minimize problems.

Give Parents Nonteaching Roles

I used to invite parents to help out by leading reading or writing conferences or running math groups. But now I strongly discourage this practice. For one thing, parents, unless they're also teachers, probably won't have the specific skills needed to do this sort of academic coaching. Also, visiting adults may be less tuned in to the sensitive nature of fourth graders than you are, and they won't know all of your students as well as you do. So they may inadvertently offer correction or well-meaning criticism in a way that feels harsh and upsetting to some children. Or, in trying to be helpful, they may overwhelm anxious fourth graders with too many things to work on at once. It's best, therefore, to invite parents to help out with special projects while doing the day-to-day instruction yourself.

Family Participation Ideas

School-Day Ideas

- Help with setup and cleanup for a special lunch or snack
- Help with messy or complicated arts and craft projects
- Chaperone field trips
- Do photocopying, stapling, etc.
- Help children learn a new board or card game

Evening Ideas

- **Poetry slam.** Students read aloud a poem they've written.
- **Science share.** Students share the science projects they've worked on in class.
- **Social studies movie night.** Families and students watch a movie based on a theme in social studies.
- **Math games night.** Students teach family members their favorite math games.
- **Reading project night.** After completing reading projects on books they've read, students share their projects with families.

Reduce or Eliminate Competition

Award ceremonies, science fairs, spelling bees . . . these and other traditional ways of sharing student achievements with families can be especially stressful for fourth graders. So instead of a science fair, where projects are judged and prizes given, consider a science share, where students showcase their learning without being judged. See "Family Participation Ideas" on page 98 for other ways that fourth graders can more comfortably share their accomplishments with their families.

If award ceremonies are expected at your school, recognize each child for a significant accomplishment (such as learning a new math formula, conducting a research project, or writing a story). These kinds of inclusive activities, in which students of all abilities and interests participate, are much more in line with the developmental needs of fourth graders. For some good ideas, see the book *Recognition without Rewards* by Caren Cameron, Colleen Politano, Daphne MacNaughton, and Betty Tate (Portage & Main, 1997).

99

Closing Thoughts

Strong school–home communication yields positive results at any grade, but it's especially helpful as children (and their parents) deal with the emotional intensity often experienced by fourth graders. By sharing information about happenings in the classroom and about typical developmental changes and characteristics in fourth graders, you make parents valued partners in the education of their children. And we know that when parents are more connected with school, children are more connected with school, becoming more fully engaged and enthusiastic learners!

Favorite Books, Board Games, and Websites
for Fourth Graders

Choosing books, games, and websites for your class is one of the most enjoyable aspects of teaching, but it can also quickly start to feel daunting because there are so many—thousands!—of great books and other resources to choose from. The following lists are starting points, with some of my personal favorites. I've tried to cover a variety of ability levels and interests. Keep in mind that my recommendations represent just a tiny fraction of all there is out there for fourth graders. Begin with these, and then have fun exploring further on your own!

Read-Aloud Books

The Adventures of Tom Sawyer by Mark Twain (Familiarize yourself with the text before reading this book aloud, and consider changing potentially inflammatory words to ones more acceptable by today's standards. This is actually wise to do with any book.)

Abuelos by Pat Mora

Beautiful Warrior by Emily Arnold McCully

Bunnicula by Deborah and James Howe

Frindle by Andrew Clements

The Girl Who Spun Gold by Virginia Hamilton

Hatchet by Gary Paulsen

Henry and the Kite Dragon by Bruce E. Hall

The Hobbit by J. R. R. Tolkien

Holes by Louis Sachar

Maniac Magee by Jerry Spinelli

Matilda by Roald Dahl

My Best Friend by Mary Ann Rodman

Number the Stars by Lois Lowry

One Grain of Rice by Demi

The Phantom Tollbooth by Norton Juster

Show Way by Jacqueline Woodson

The Unbreakable Code by Sara Hoagland Hunter

Where the Red Fern Grows by Wilson Rawls

A Wrinkle in Time by Madeleine L'Engle

Classroom Library Books

All the read-alouds I listed are great for the classroom library. In addition, consider these favorites:

Fiction

American Girl (series) by multiple authors

Animorphs (series) by K. A. Applegate

Baseball Card Adventures (series) by Dan Gutman

Because of Winn-Dixie by Kate DiCamillo

The Boxcar Children (series) by Gertrude Chandler Warner and others

Captain Underpants (series) by Dav Pilkey

Crossing Bok Chitto: A Choctaw Tale of Friendship and Freedom by Tim Tingle

Elijah of Buxton by Christopher Curtis

The Enormous Egg by Oliver Butterworth

Esperanza Rising by Pam Muñoz Ryan

How to Eat Fried Worms by Thomas Rockwell

The Incredible Journey by Sheila Burnford

Little House on the Prairie (series) by Laura Ingalls Wilder

The Hungry Coat: A Tale from Turkey by Demi

Project Mulberry by Linda Sue Park

Ralph S. Mouse by Beverly Cleary

Red Ridin' in the Hood and Other Cuentos by Patricia Santos Marcantonio

The Red Rose Box by Brenda Woods

Safe at Home by Sharon Robinson

The Spiderwick Chronicles (series) by Holly Black and Tony DiTerlizzi

Stuart Little by E. B. White

Tales of a Fourth Grade Nothing by Judy Blume

Time Warp Trio (series) by Jon Scieszka

The Trouble Begins by Linda Himelblau

Wayside School (series) by Louis Sachar

The Year of the Dog by Grace Lin

Poetry

Angels Ride Bikes and Other Fall Poems by Francisco X. Alarcon

Joyful Noise: Poems for Two Voices by Paul Fleischman

A Light in the Attic by Shel Silverstein

My Man Blue by Nikki Grimes

Ordinary Things by Ralph Fletcher, illustrated by Walter Lyon Krudop

Where the Sidewalk Ends by Shel Silverstein

Informational Texts and Other Nonfiction

Almost Astronauts: 13 Women Who Dared to Dream by Tanya Lee Stone

Childhood of Famous Americans (series) from Aladdin Paperbacks

Eyewitness Books from DK Publishing

Graphic Science (series) by Capstone Press

Highlights magazine

Kakapo Rescue: Saving the World's Strangest Parrot by Sy Montgomery

Librarian of Basra: A True Story from Iraq by Jeanette Winter

Ranger Rick magazine

Science for Every Kid (series) from Wiley

Sixteen Years, Sixteen Seconds: The Sammy Lee Story by Paula Yoo

The Snake Scientist by Sy Montgomery, illustrated by Nic Bishop

We Are the Ship: The Story of Negro League Baseball by Kadir Nelson

Adding to Your Class or School Library

To find additional books and authors, talk with other teachers, librarians, parents—and the children themselves. These websites are also a great resource for expanding any library:

New York Public Library:
Best Books for Children
KIDS.NYPL.ORG/READING/RECOMMENDED.CFM

Association for Library Service to Children (ALSC):
Caldecott Medal Books
WWW.ALA.ORG/ALA/MGRPS/DIVS/ALSC/AWARDSGRANTS/BOOKMEDIA/
CALDECOTTMEDAL/CALDECOTTMEDAL.CFM

National Council for the Social Studies (NCSS):
Notable Tradebooks for Young People
WWW.SOCIALSTUDIES.ORG/RESOURCES/NOTABLE

Board/Card Games

Checkers

Chinese Checkers

Mad Gab (Mattel)

Mancala

Othello

Pay Day (Winning Moves Games)

Parcheesi

Rummikub (Pressman)

Set (SET Enterprises)

Spill and Spell (Endless Games)

UNO (Mattel)

Yahtzee (Hasbro)

Websites

Math Is Fun! ■ WWW.MATHISFUN.COM A site chock-full of games, puzzles, and reference information on a variety of math content strands.

National Wildlife Federation Kids ■ WWW.NWF.ORG/KIDS.ASPX This site offers tons of information and activities about the natural world in a kid-friendly format.

National Geographic Kids ■ WWW.KIDS.NATIONALGEOGRAPHIC.COM An interactive website with activities, games, and animal information.

NASA Kids' Club ■ WWW.NASA.GOV/AUDIENCE/FORKIDS/KIDSCLUB/FLASH/ A website all about outer space.

netTrekker ■ WWW.NETTREKKER.COM This educational search engine allows students to research science and social studies topics independently since all sites on it have been approved for student use. Requires a subscription.

VocabularySpellingCity ■ WWW.SPELLINGCITY.COM Users can create personalized spelling and word games according to word lists.

About the *Responsive Classroom®* Approach

All of the recommended practices in this book come from or are consistent with *Responsive Classroom®*, an evidence-based education approach associated with greater teacher effectiveness, higher student achievement, and improved school climate. *Responsive Classroom* practices help educators build competencies in four interrelated domains: engaging academics, positive community, effective management, and developmentally appropriate teaching.

To learn more about the *Responsive Classroom* approach, see the following resources published by Center for Responsive Schools and available from www.responsiveclassroom.org • 800-360-6332.

Morning Meeting: Gather as a whole class each morning to greet each other, share news, and warm up for the day of learning ahead.

> *The Morning Meeting Book*, 3rd ed., by Roxann Kriete and Carol Davis. 2014.
>
> *80 Morning Meeting Ideas for Grades K–2* by Susan Lattanzi Roser. 2012.
>
> *80 Morning Meeting Ideas for Grades 3–6* by Carol Davis. 2012.
>
> *99 Activities and Greetings: Great for Morning Meeting ... and other meetings, too!* by Melissa Correa-Connolly. 2004.
>
> *Doing Math in Morning Meeting: 150 Quick Activities That Connect to Your Curriculum* by Andy Dousis and Margaret Berry Wilson. 2010.
>
> *Doing Science in Morning Meeting: 150 Quick Activities That Connect to Your Curriculum* by Lara Webb and Margaret Berry Wilson. 2013.
>
> *Doing Language Arts in Morning Meeting: 150 Quick Activities That Connect to Your Curriculum* by Jodie Luongo, Joan Riordan, and Kate Umstatter. 2015.
>
> *Doing Social Studies in Morning Meeting: 150 Quick Activities That Connect to Your Curriculum* by Leah Carson and Jane Cofie. 2017.
>
> *Morning Meeting* Professional Development Kit. 2008.

Positive Teacher Language: Use words and tone as a tool to promote children's active learning, sense of community, and self-discipline.

The Power of Our Words: Teacher Language That Helps Children Learn, 2nd ed., by Paula Denton, EdD. 2014.

Teacher Language for Engaged Learning: 4 Video Study Sessions. 2013.

Teacher Language Professional Development Kit. 2010.

Engaging Academics: Learn tools for effective teaching and making lessons lively, appropriately challenging, and purposeful to help children develop higher levels of motivation, persistence, and mastery of skills and content.

The Language of Learning: Teaching Students Core Thinking, Speaking, and Listening Skills by Margaret Berry Wilson. 2014.

The Joyful Classroom: Practical Ways to Engage and Challenge Students K–6. From *Responsive Classroom.* 2016.

Special Area Educators: Explore key *Responsive Classroom* practices adapted for a wide variety of special areas.

Responsive Classroom for Music, Art, PE, and Other Special Areas. From *Responsive Classroom.* 2017.

Foundation-Setting During the First Weeks of School: Take time in the critical first weeks of school to establish expectations, routines, a sense of community, and a positive classroom tone.

The First Six Weeks of School, 2nd ed. From *Responsive Classroom.* 2015.

Teaching Discipline: Use practical strategies, such as rule creation and positive responses to misbehavior, to promote self-discipline in students and build a safe, calm, and respectful school climate.

Teasing, Tattling, Defiance and More: Positive Approaches to 10 Common Classroom Behaviors by Margaret Berry Wilson. 2013.

Rules in School: Teaching Discipline in the Responsive Classroom, 2nd ed., by Kathryn Brady, Mary Beth Forton, and Deborah Porter. 2011.

Responsive School Discipline: Essentials for Elementary School Leaders by Chip Wood and Babs Freeman-Loftis. 2011.

Teaching Discipline in the Classroom Professional Development Kit. 2011.

Classroom Management: Set up and run a classroom in ways that enable the best possible teaching and learning.

Interactive Modeling: A Powerful Technique for Teaching Children by Margaret Berry Wilson. 2012.

Teaching Children to Care: Classroom Management for Ethical and Academic Growth K–8, rev. ed., by Ruth Sidney Charney. 2002.

Movement, Games, Songs, and Chants: Sprinkle quick, lively activities throughout the school day to keep students energized, engaged, and alert.

Closing Circles: 50 Activities for Ending the Day in a Positive Way by Dana Januszka and Kristen Vincent. 2012.

99 Activities and Greetings: Great for Morning Meeting ... and other meetings, too! by Melissa Correa-Connolly. 2004.

Energizers! 88 Quick Movement Activities That Refresh and Refocus, K–6 by Susan Lattanzi Roser. 2009..

Preventing Bullying at School: Use practical strategies throughout the day to create a safe, kind environment in which bullying is far less likely to take root

How to Bullyproof Your Classroom by Caltha Crowe. 2012. (Includes bullying prevention lessons.)

Solving Behavior Problems With Children: Engage children in solving their behavior problems so they feel safe, challenged, and invested in changing.

Solving Thorny Behavior Problems: How Teachers and Students Can Work Together by Caltha Crowe. 2009.

Sammy and His Behavior Problems: Stories and Strategies from a Teacher's Year by Caltha Crowe. 2010.

Teasing, Tattling, Defiance and More: Positive Approaches to 10 Common Classroom Behaviors by Margaret Berry Wilson. 2013.

Child Development: Understand children's common physical, social-emotional, cognitive, and language characteristics at each age, and adapt teaching to respond to children's developmental needs.

Yardsticks: Child and Adolescent Development Ages 4–14, 4th ed., by Chip Wood. 2018.

Child Development Pamphlet Series (based on *Yardsticks* by Chip Wood). Available for grades K–8.

Professional Development/Staff Meetings: Learn easy-to-use structures for getting the most out of your work with colleagues.

Energize Your Meetings! 35 Interactive Learning Structures for Educators. 2014.

About Child Development

Understanding children's development is crucial to teaching them well. To learn more about child development, see the following resources:

Child and Adolescent Development for Educators by Michael Pressley and Christine McCormick. Guilford Press. 2007. This textbook presents understandable explanations of theories and research about child development and suggests ways to apply those theories and research to classroom teaching.

Child Development, 8th ed., by Laura E. Berk. Pearson Education, Inc. 2009. This textbook summarizes the history and current thinking about child development in easy-to-understand prose. The author outlines the major theories and research and provides practical guidance for teachers.

Child Development Guide by the Center for Development of Human Services, SUNY, Buffalo State College. WWW.BSC-CDHS.ORG/FOSTER PARENTTRAINING/PDFS/CHILDDEVELGUIDE.PDF. The center presents characteristics of children at each stage of development in an easy-to-use guide for foster parents.

"The Child in the Elementary School" by Frederick C. Howe in *Child Study Journal*, Vol. 23, Issue 4. 1993. The author presents the common characteristics of students at each grade level, identified by observing students and gathering teacher observations.

"How the Brain Learns: Growth Cycles of Brain and Mind" by Kurt W. Fischer and Samuel P. Rose in *Educational Leadership*, Vol. 56: 3, pp. 56–60. November 1998. The authors, who blend the study of child development with neuroscience, summarize their prior work in a format intended for educators. They conclude that "both behavior and the brain change in repeating patterns that seem to involve common growth cycles."

"The Scientist in the Crib: A Conversation with Andrew Meltzoff" by Marcia D'Arcangelo in *Educational Leadership*, Vol. 58: 3, pp. 8–13. November 2000. In an interview format, this article dispels myths about child development and explores ways in which research about cognitive development might inform the work of educators.

Yardsticks: Child and Adolescent Development Ages 4–14, 4th ed., by Chip Wood. Center for Responsive Schools. 2018. This highly practical book for teachers and parents offers narratives and easy-to-scan charts of children's common physical, social-emotional, cognitive, and language characteristics at each age from four through fourteen and notes how these growth patterns relate to learning.

Your Child: Emotional, Behavioral, and Cognitive Development from Birth through Preadolescence by AACAP (American Academy of Child and Adolescent Psychiatry) and David Pruitt. Harper Paperbacks. 2000. Intended for parents, this book presents information about children's development and common characteristics of each age, and offers tips for helping children develop appropriately.

ACKNOWLEDGMENTS

This book, as I suspect is the case with nearly all books, was a collaborative effort. In some ways, it began as I began my teaching career and found myself immersed in the joyful and sometimes confusing world of teaching fourth grade. I'd like to thank many of my early colleagues for helping me get off to a good start, especially Nancy Moretta, Gail Schatz, Andy Dousis, Peter Bass, Mike Guarraia, and Cherry McLaughlin. With such supportive, nurturing, and playful colleagues, it was easy to be excited and inspired as a new teacher.

I'd also like to thank the amazing team of professionals at Northeast Foundation for Children, who continue to guide and inspire me. Margaret Berry Wilson, Alice Yang, and Elizabeth Nash were especially important in the development of this text. Thanks for all of the lively debate and important questions. And Helen Merena deserves special thanks for creating such an appealing design for this book. [Publisher's note: Northeast Foundation for Children is the former name of Center for Responsive Schools.]

I'm also very appreciative of Marissa Hutter for her insights when reviewing the manuscript.

Finally, and most important, I would like to thank my wife, Heather, and my children, Ethan and Carly, for keeping me grounded and sane.

111

ABOUT THE AUTHOR

Mike Anderson taught third, fourth, and fifth grades for fifteen years before becoming a *Responsive Classroom®* consultant, leading teacher workshops and consulting with schools on using the *Responsive Classroom* approach. In 2004, he was the recipient of a Milken National Educator Award for excellence in teaching.

Mike is the author of two other books in the *What Every Teacher Needs to Know* series (third grade and fifth grade) and is a co-author of *The First Six Weeks of School*, all published by Center for Responsive Schools. He is also the author of *The Well-Balanced Teacher* (ASCD, 2010) and co-author of *The Research-Ready Classroom* (Heinemann, 2006). Mike lives in Durham, New Hampshire, with his wife, Heather, and their two children, Ethan and Carly.